Maggie
my stars can
+ wither for
too when
is dead.
love
Gran

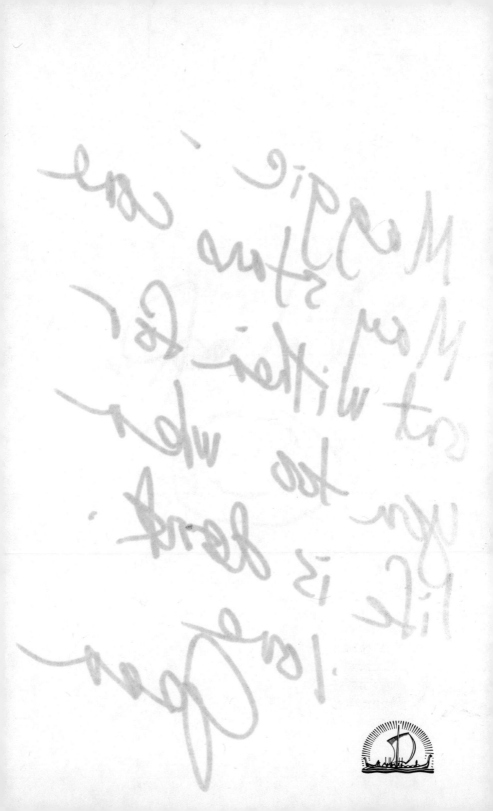

Maggie -
May stars come
out within for
you too when
life is dark.
love Joan

STARS
COME OUT
WITHIN

JEAN LITTLE

VIKING

VIKING
Published by the Penguin Group
Penguin Books Canada Ltd, 10 Alcorn Avenue, Toronto,
Ontario, Canada M4V 3B2
Penguin Books Ltd, 27 Wrights Lane, London W8 5TZ, England
Viking Penguin, a division of Penguin Books USA Inc.,
375 Hudson Street, New York, New York, 10014, U.S.A.
Penguin Books Australia Ltd, Ringwood, Victoria, Australia
Penguin Books (NZ) Ltd, 182-190 Wairau Road,
Auckland 10, New Zealand

Penguin Books Ltd, Registered Offices: Harmondsworth,
Middlesex, England

First published 1990

3 5 7 9 10 8 6 4 2

Copyright © Jean Little, 1990

Printed and bound in the United States of America
on acid-free paper ∞

Canadian Cataloguing in Publication Data

Little, Jean, 1932–
Stars come out within

ISBN 0-670-82965-X

1. Little, Jean, 1932–   —Biography.
2. Novelists, Canadian (English) — 20th century —
Biography.*   3. Visually handicapped — Canada —
Biography.   I. Title.
PS8523.I87Z53 1990   C813'.54 C90-094164-2
PR9199.3.L57Z47 1990

American Library of Congress Cataloguing in
Publication Data Available

Claire Mackay

This book is for Jenny Stephens, Claire Mackay
and Katherine Paterson, who know how to
make light of darkness.

PROLOGUE

In 1862, Emily Dickinson wrote a poem about me.

It began, "We grow accustomed to the dark . . ." I have taken my title from the last line in the third verse. I had to alter it slightly. Yet, as anyone who has read her letters knows, Emily herself found that, eventually, stars do come out within.

Since her poem contains the heart of my story, I will quote it in its entirety here. Her words have helped me "meet the Road erect."

> *We grow accustomed to the Dark—*
> *When Light is put away—*
> *As when the Neighbor holds the Lamp*
> *To witness her Goodbye—*
>
> *A Moment—We uncertain step*
> *For newness of the night—*
> *Then—fit our Vision to the Dark—*
> *And meet the Road—erect—*
>
> *And so of larger—Darknesses—*
> *Those Evenings of the Brain—*
> *When not a Moon disclose a sign—*
> *Or Star—come out—within—*
>
> *The B[r]avest—grope a little—*
> *And sometimes hit a Tree*
> *Directly in the Forehead—*
> *But as they learn to see—*

Either the Darkness alters—
Or something in the sight
Adjusts itself to Midnight—
And Life steps almost straight.

This poem meant even more to me when I learned that Emily Dickinson suffered from an eye ailment herself. Cynthia Griffin Wolff, in her recent biography of the poet, suggests that when Emily Dickinson wrote to Thomas Higginson the often quoted passage, "I had a terror—since September—I could tell to none—so I sing as the Boy does by the Burying Ground—because I am afraid," she might well have been talking about her fear of becoming blind. The words certainly reflect my own terror of losing my vision.

I have always enjoyed books in which each chapter begins with an apt quotation. As I worked on this manuscript, I found bits of other Emily Dickinson poems popping into my mind, beginning with "I'm Nobody! Who are You? . . ." That went so perfectly with my second chapter. When I searched through her poems—1,175 of them—I discovered others equally satisfying. Choosing which lines to use as chapter headings was the most enjoyable part of writing this book.

My thanks go to the poet and also to the many people who helped collect her scribbles of poetry, written on scraps of brown paper and the backs of envelopes, and get them into print for me and for everyone else who reads her work with wonder and delight.

As in my previous autobiographical book, *Little by Little: A Writer's Education*, I have tried to tell my story as it seemed to me while I was living it. This does away with the necessity to keep apologizing for my naivete, pride and self-pity. I trust the reader will perceive such character flaws unaided by my hindsight.

Many people who are dear to me will not find themselves in these pages. This is chiefly because they have been my friends rather than my teachers or rescuers.

Is the book true? I did my best to make it so. But Emily Dickinson gave me this instruction:

> *Tell all the Truth but tell it slant—*
> *Success in Circuit lies*
> *Too bright for our infirm Delight*
> *The Truth's superb surprise*

Have I told all? No. I have tried to tell about those incidents and relationships that have added to my education as a blind Canadian woman who writes books for children. Emily Dickinson also told me something about memory which I found helpful.

> *Remembrance has a Rear and Front—*
> *Tis something like a House—*
> *It has a Garret also*
> *For Refuse and the Mouse.*

Although I'll take you into my house of memory, I won't give you a tour of every room, and I'll try to keep out of that attic. Be thankful.

Jean Little
Guelph, 1990

1

There is no Frigate like a Book
To take us Lands away
Nor any Coursers like a Page
Of prancing Poetry—
          Emily Dickinson

"Jeanie," Rose Vanderweit, the nursing assistant at the Crippled Children's Centre, shrieked. "Look at your shoes! You've got on one blue and one brown."

"Stop teasing," I said and looked down at my feet. Even I could not have come to school on my very first teaching day wearing mismatched shoes.

She was right. I had dressed in the dark, hoping to fool myself into believing that I need not go through this first day of being a schoolteacher. Groping for my shoes, I had forgotten that my brown Brevitts had been so comfortable, I had recently bought a twin pair in blue.

If only I had begun teaching in September like everyone else! Then the sun would have been up before me. But it had taken me all fall to find my students, explain the program to their families and transform the great empty space at the Guelph Crippled Children's Centre into a well-equipped and welcoming classroom.

"In winter, I get up at night," Robert Louis Stevenson had written in *A Child's Garden of Verses*. He was not the only one. But why hadn't Mother checked me over? I raced to the phone.

1

"I'll be right there," said my repentant parent.

I hung up, praying that the children would be late. God was not listening. Before Mother could possibly have had time to drive across town, I heard the first carload pulling up. Rose laughed as I tucked one foot behind the other and swivelled to face the door, feeling far more crippled than any of the five boys I was about to welcome.

In they came — Clifford, Billy and Max on crutches, Barry walking with the painful slowness of a child with muscular dystrophy and, last in line, five-year-old Alec with his wild ataxic stagger. Automatically stepping forward to catch hold of him, I forgot my odd shoes. Like Bill and Clifford, he had cerebral palsy but could not balance well enough to walk without help. As I grabbed his flailing arms and supported him, he looked up at me.

He was a funny-looking little boy. Except for one rebellious cowlick, his sandy hair flopped down over his forehead. His ears stuck straight out like cup handles. He was skinny, all sharp elbows and spindly, spidery legs. His eyes, raised to meet mine, looked serious.

Then he smiled. It was like the sun coming up over the edge of the world and flooding the land with light.

"Good morning, Miss Little," he said.

Miss Little! The respect he put into that simple title changed me. His words struck exactly the ceremonious note I needed. This five-year-old with a smile like sunrise knew who I was. I was not a scared twenty-six-year-old who was certain she was going to forget "God Save the Queen." I was his teacher.

I unwound his long scarf and helped him out of his coat. As I got him settled in his desk, Mother arrived with my other brown shoe. I jammed it on my foot with all the children watching.

"I can't see well," I heard myself telling them, "and this morning I didn't turn on the light when I was getting dressed . . ."

Mother left. The boys sized me up. Then they laughed. But their laughter was kind. They, too, often had difficulty dressing.

Clifford cleared his throat. Blushing scarlet, he said, "If you don't mind my asking, Miss Little, what happened to your eyes?"

Soft-hearted Billy tried to shush him, but the rest waited for my reaction. It was right that they should be told. After all, I knew all about them, didn't I?

"I don't mind," I patted Bill's shoulder. He beamed up at me. Alec's smile had been like sunrise; Billy's was like high noon.

"I was born blind," I said.

They gasped. Blind!

"But I don't remember being blind," I continued.

"Did you have an operation?" they asked. They knew about operations. Each of them had spent time in doctors' offices and hospitals. All knew kids who had been helped by surgery.

"No operation," I said. "My eyes were scarred somehow before I was born. Nobody knows exactly how. But after I was born, the scars shrank a bit and my eyes grew so that before I turned two, my parents realized I was starting to see after all."

"They must have been happy," Max commented. He sounded interested but a little impatient. He wanted to start learning.

"Why . . . well, what I mean is . . . your eyes . . .?" Cliff struggled to ask why I was cross-eyed, but could not find polite words.

"My eyes cross because I only use one at a time," I explained. "I can't look through both at once. One of my pupils, the little black holes you see through, is higher than the other so the pictures they make are too different to fuse into one."

They looked puzzled, so I drew a diagram of the human eye on the board. Part of my mind was telling me that we had not yet sung "God Save the Queen." But the teacher I was becoming dismissed the rigidity of schedules. Everyone in my class was learning plenty, even Max. We'd get around to the Queen.

"So," I finished, "when I use my right eye, it sees you, but my left one, which I'm not using, slides over by my nose and waits till I need it. I can switch back and forth. Watch."

As I looked through one eye and then the other, they first stared and then giggled. Barry spoke up for the first time.

"Your eyes sort of . . . jiggle," he observed. "I mean, even when you are looking at us, the one eye kind of . . . keeps wobbling."

A positive shriek of laughter greeted this perfectly accurate observation. I nodded at Barry.

"That's called nystagmus," I told him. "The proper word for 'crossed eyes' is strabismus."

I remembered being a disabled child. It had helped me a lot to learn the clinical terms that described my condition. Did these boys know how to tell others about their diagnoses? I asked them.

Max did. He had not had Legg Perthes for long. The others had heard the words "cerebral palsy" and "muscular dystrophy" but could not pronounce them correctly or use them with confidence. I taught each child an impressive string of diagnostic terms to use when he needed them. They were enchanted with this accomplishment.

Billy, for instance, was soon able to rhyme off, "I have cerebral palsy. I'm a spastic quadraplegic."

Later I myself heard Barry silence a couple of insensitive student nurses who were speculating in loud whispers about what ailed him. "I have childhood muscular dystrophy," he informed them. "There's no cure for it yet but they are doing research."

"Miss Little, how far can you see?" Alec asked.

"I can see as far as the sun," I said solemnly. Then I told him what he really wanted to know. "I can see the same things you can — the walls, the windows, you, Rose, the easel. But I can't tell what colour your eyes are. I can see trees out that window, but I can't see separate leaves. I can read, but only if I hold the book up close. When I was a little girl, my mum was always sending me to wash the printer's ink off my nose — especially if I'd been reading comic books."

At last I began trying to follow my carefully prepared lesson plans. But before we embarked on the curriculum, my five students had learned dignified adult words with which to talk about themselves, and they had discovered that they were not the only people with disabilities. And I had found that some of the best teaching is done when you are following your instinct rather than the lessons you spent so much time preparing. I had also seen a boy whom I had been informed had "only a 40 I.Q." memorize the medical terminology for his disability without effort.

The boys now felt free to share with me the embarrassing moments they had experienced. They also began watching for opportunities to help me. It soon became clear that while they needed me to help them move about the room or use their hands, I needed them to find what I lost and see what I missed.

Children came and went at the Centre. Max recovered from his crippling condition and departed. Others went to hospital for surgery and then returned. Finally a girl joined the class. Some of the kids progressed slowly towards greater independence. Barry, and later his younger brother, Randy, had to live with a progressive disease that made them steadily weaker.

"It must be so depressing teaching those poor kids," people who did not know them often said. "I don't see how you bear it."

But I was not teaching "those poor kids"; I was working with Billy, Ellen, Cliff, Barry and Alec. I lost my temper at them. I laughed with them. I taught them songs and stories. I tripped over their crutches. I helped them earn enough money to buy two guinea pigs and took them to the pet store to choose them. We flew kites and went to the circus, the zoo, a hockey game and a fall fair. We took bus and train rides. I invented a dangerous but exciting game called Crutch Ball. I worked hard at teaching them to read. They corrected my arithmetic. We were too busy to get depressed.

Since Alec was ataxic, his sense of balance was faulty. He would pull himself to his feet, aim his body at a chair or bookcase and launch himself through space. He would go careening across to it, waving his arms wildly and, just in time, clutch at its support. When he did not quite make it he went sprawling, but he was practised at falling and never did himself lasting damage.

Every day Rose would take each of the kids out of class to physio- and occupational therapy. There they would do a succession of exercises to help them gain mobility and some daily living skills. In Alec's case they worked on his sense of balance. One afternoon he asked the physiotherapist when he could begin to use crutches. She said he could start to practise balancing that very day, found him crutches that fitted him and stood him correctly with one under each armpit.

"Now just stand and get used to them for a bit," she said, turning to another task. "You'll need lots of practice."

When she next turned around, Alec was walking away, moving his left foot and his right crutch together and then, the next moment, swinging his right crutch and his left foot forward. He had not studied Clifford and Billy for nothing. She gawked at him and then rushed to call the rest of us.

In seconds, all of us who could get there were in the hall watching the miracle. It was not a cure, but it seemed every bit as dramatic and splendid to us. It was Alec's first experience of being in control of his own mobility. Never again would he have to depend on convenient pieces of furniture and outstretched hands. Alec, before our eyes, was taking his first true steps. From now on, if he could complete this journey, he would be choosing his own path. Slowly and steadily, with immense concentration, he came swinging down the long hall towards the classroom.

"See the beads of sweat on his forehead," somebody whispered.

When he reached the door, the children still in their desks cheered. Even Barry, who had been walking when he came to the Centre but was now in a wheelchair, was beaming.

"Hey, Alec," he called, "that's showing them, boy!"

Alec did not turn his head or even smile. He was concentrating every muscle, every nerve, every thought on this immense undertaking. When he finally reached his own desk, he swivelled his body, carefully lowered himself onto the seat and took his two crutches and stowed them out of harm's way on the floor. He gave a tired sigh and, finally, looked at our exultant faces. Self-conscious though it was, his grin left me dazzled.

"You're shaking, Alec," said Margaret Bryant, Rose's replacement.

"So would you be if you'd done what he's just done," the therapist told her. She blew her nose like a trumpet.

She was not the only one whose eyes were wet.

After school we all crammed into the therapist's car and went home with Alec. Before she honked the horn to let his mother know we had arrived, we stood him up with a crutch under each arm. As his mother came out onto the doorstep, she saw her son come walking up the sidewalk, on his own two feet for the first time in his life.

Mrs Arnett took one look at him, gave a strangled sob and sat down hard on the step. Then, not caring if all the world saw her, she buried her face in her hands and burst into tears. Once again the kids were cheering. Once again we adults were fishing in our pockets for Kleenexes.

I had begun to teach with very little training. After nearly three years of teaching, I took some time off to become fully qualified. Before returning to the Centre I wrote the first draft of a children's book called *Mine for Keeps*. It was the story of ten-year-old Sally Copeland who happened to have cerebral palsy.

I wanted to try writing a novel. My students loved Anne Shirley of Green Gables, Pooh and Piglet, Henry

Huggins of Klickitat Street, Heidi, and Dorothy and Toto of Oz. Yet I felt strongly that somewhere among this throng of beloved heroes and heroines there should be at least one thoroughly real child who had to use crutches or was in a wheelchair like my kids. I had found a few disabled fictional children: Jimmy Bean in *Pollyanna*, Clara in *Heidi*, Prince Dolor in *The Little Lame Prince*, invalidish Carol Bird in *The Birds' Christmas Carol*. But my class and I had discovered that in almost every case, boys and girls who started out crippled invariably ended up either dying like Beth in *Little Women* or being cured miraculously like Colin Craven in *The Secret Garden*. The kids were puzzled by these outcomes. I thought them insulting. Why couldn't any of these authors imagine a happy ending that was honest? Did they, deep down, believe that you could not remain disabled and have a full, joyful life? If that was it, they were crazy. *Mine for Keeps*, with Sally still on crutches at the finish, was my answer to their lack of imagination.

I returned to teach at the Centre, but I continued working on my book when I could. Once it was done, I entered it in the Little, Brown Canadian Children's Book Competition.

Then, while I waited for results, I worked both at teaching and at preparing myself for the inevitable rejection letter. Every writer I had read about had insisted that no first book gets accepted on its initial trip to a publisher's office. Even Dr Seuss, a great favourite with my students, was said to have had his first book turned down more than twenty times.

Yet no matter how I tried not to hope, an intrepid little voice inside me kept saying, "It's good. Even if they don't give it the prize, they might take it if you agree to do more work."

In May the letter came. They not only wanted to publish it; they were actually giving me the money!

The morning after this bombshell struck, I had a hard time keeping my mind on teaching. As I assigned pages of arithmetic and heard my scholars read, I kept staring into space and smiling goofily. The children, who had heard the story in manuscript and who had seen the incredible letter now in my pocket, exchanged amused glances as I overlooked blatant errors.

"Four nines are twenty-seven," Janice said.

"Very good, Janice," I replied dreamily.

When the older children exploded into peals of laughter, I was taken completely by surprise. As the little ones joined in, I replayed the exchange and felt my cheeks grow pink.

Should I claim I had done it on purpose, just to see whether they were alert? One look at their gleeful faces told me that, this time, they could not be hoodwinked.

"Put your work away," I said with dignity. "It's lunchtime."

After lunch, Margaret helped me unstack the canvas cots and get the kids onto them. Then the children quieted, waiting for me to start reading a new book.

Even though they ranged in age from six to thirteen, I read aloud to the whole group every day at this hour. This was supposed to take about thirty minutes but had been known to stretch to an hour on days when a good story had us in its grip.

The day before we had finished the last Mary Poppins story.

Even knowing how much the kids enjoyed all kinds of books, I had been astonished by their devotion to P.L. Travers' redoubtable magic nanny. When I had finished reading the first book about this personage, they had insisted on going on to its sequels. And the day before, when I had closed *Mary Poppins Opens the Door* and had had to tell them that there were no more books about her, Alec had flabbergasted everyone by beginning to cry.

Janice had saved the day. "Miss Little, Mary Poppins bought a Return Ticket," she had said. "You only do that if you're coming back."

"That's true," I had said gratefully.

"The lady is probably working on another book right this minute," Laurie had put in.

Nobody mentioned Mary Poppins now; nobody looked at Alec. Yet I could feel their wistfulness. They wanted that faraway, adventure-filled, yet totally safe world.

I myself could hardly wait to begin sharing *Warrior Scarlet* by Rosemary Sutcliff with them. The week before, I had stayed up half the night reading it. She, too, had written about a disabled kid who remained handicapped to the end. I was certain that my class, as they listened, would share my sense of affirmation. The Bronze Age hero, Drem, has one useless arm. My kids had far more in common with him than they did with Mary Poppins.

The language was not easy for them to grasp at first. Even when Drem's grandfather barked, "Think you the young one will ever win his way into the Men's Side, with a spear-arm that he cannot use?" most of the kids missed the meaning of his speech. I did not stop to explain. They would catch on before long.

They remained dreamy, drowsy, until we came to these words:

. . . *he looked at his right arm as though he had*

never seen it before: his spear arm that he could not use, the Grandfather had said. It was thinner than his left, and somehow brittle-looking, as though it might snap like a dry stick. He felt it exploringly with his left hand. It was queer, like something that did not quite belong to him. He had always known, of course — when he thought about it at all — that he couldn't use that arm, but it hadn't seemed important. He held things in his teeth and he held things between his knees, and he managed well enough without it. . . .

"It's like Paddy's," someone whispered. I paused momentarily and looked at the children. Six-year-old Paddy, who did indeed have just such an arm, was sitting up straight by the time I finished. Brian was feeling his crippled hand, checking to see if it felt like Drem's. Nobody interrupted but not one of them was sleepy any longer. My class had taken on Drem's fight for acceptance, recognizing it as their own. When Drem failed his wolf-slaying, the entire class was sniffling. When, later, he did win his Warrior Scarlet, every child in the room triumphed with him.

Walking home that night, I thought about Janice's faith in Mary Poppins' Return Ticket. Would children ever hope I was writing a sequel? Would they want another book about the Copelands?

That mattered far more to me than the one-thousand-dollar prize. I hoped some day to give up teaching to become a writer. Some people managed to combine the jobs, but I knew that I could not. Each needed my full attention, my whole heart, all my skill.

But how would the children I so loved get along without me?

I had it backwards. My students, like Drem, were

tough as well as vulnerable. They would survive and, even, triumph.

The real question was how would I get along without them. Just the thought of leaving them made my heart ache.

I did not yet know that they would never desert me, that one or more of them would sneak into every book I would some day write, that every one of my students was mine for keeps.

2

I'm Nobody! Who are you?
Are you—Nobody—too?
Emily Dickinson

"Miss Little, will you bring the money to school so we can see?" Paddy called from the taxi. "I've never seen a thousand dollars."

Before I could answer, the cab pulled away. I laughed. Did the kids imagine that I was going to come back from the Canadian Authors Association Awards banquet with a sack of coins or a stack of crackling dollar bills? Or had the older ones, at least, realized that this fortune would come in a small insignificant-looking slip of paper?

Yet as Mother and I headed into Howard Ferguson Hall for the CAA Awards dinner, I felt as excited as Paddy had sounded. The award was not just any "piece of paper"; it was my passport into the world of Writers. I was one now with L. M. Montgomery, P. L. Travers and Rosemary Sutcliff — or I would be next spring when my book was due to be published. Tonight I might sit beside Hugh MacLennan or Gwethalyn Graham or Morley Callaghan and . . .

We entered just behind three women who were chattering as though they had all known each other from the cradle. I was so busy trying to decide whether they were authors that I tripped over the step and, clutching Mother's elbow, barely saved myself from landing flat on my face. I was thankful it was dim in the entry, as I could feel myself turning scarlet. Mother gave my cold hand a comforting squeeze. Then the two of us stood gazing around, uncertain what to do next.

Nobody noticed us. The hall was packed with people to whom we were clearly invisible. I felt my blush subsiding as we were caught up in a throng and swept forward. I went on straining my ears, eager to listen in on the talk of Canadian Authors. After all, these must be my colleagues. I longed for scraps of meaningful conversation, talk about royalty cheques, first drafts, editors and plots. Instead they seemed to be discussing their summer plans, the cost of plumbing, a new TV, their tedious children.

Surely these must be gate-crashers! Writers could not sound so utterly ordinary, could they?

Clinging to my illusions, I decided that they must let other people come to the banquet. Husbands and wives maybe. I hoped I didn't end up sitting beside some writer's relation. Yet I could not complain since I had brought my mother along.

"This is Jean Little," she said then, drawing me forward to meet a short, unhappy-looking man whose name I failed to catch.

If only I weren't cross-eyed!

Knowing he was disconcerted by my seeming not to be looking at him, I smiled warmly in the right direction. He shifted his gaze to a point over my right shoulder.

"Yes. Hello, Miss Little," he said. "I'm glad you got here without any trouble. You'll be sitting with the people from McClelland and Stewart. I'm afraid they haven't arrived yet. If you'll just come along over here. They should be along any minute."

He started to shepherd us across the room but, when we were halfway, someone called to him. Mother and I kept going till we reached the far wall. Another woman was standing there, looking as though she felt as out of place as we did. I eyed her curiously. Could she possibly be as nervous as she appeared? If she were even half as scared as she looked, she must be a beginner like me. She was alone.

I smiled, cleared my throat and spoke to her.

"I'm Jean Little," I said. Then I rushed to explain my right to be there. "I'm here to win an award for my first book. It's going to be published next spring. It's called *Mine for Keeps."*

"That's great!" the woman said. Although she still sounded panic-stricken, she also sounded as though the knowledge that I was winning a prize gave her real delight. I had a strange feeling that, for once, my peculiar eyes had scarcely been noticed. She went on in a warm, slightly husky voice that shook only a little. "I'm Margaret Laurence. I'm winning something, too. Did they say you had to make a speech?"

"Mr McClelland said to be ready to say a few words," I told her, scrabbling around inside my head for my three sentences.

"He said I didn't have to say anything," she said, as though that assurance was all that kept her from fleeing. "I don't know why they aren't here. That table had a McClelland and Stewart sign on it but it's disappeared. I think the Press have commandeered it. They're probably having one more round of cocktails."

Was she talking about the reporters or the people from McClelland and Stewart? It was nice that we had the same Canadian publisher. Every seat I could see had been taken. Someone said grace. Chairs scraped back. Tomato juice glasses were raised.

I could not believe this was happening. Here I was at the grand dinner I had been picturing to myself for days. Here I was actually in attendance at the sort of function that is every beginning writer's dream. Here I was, standing with my mother, this unknown author and one or two other people, backed up against a wall watching everybody else starting to eat. How could they?

Another woman made her way through the crowd towards us. When I learned that she was Claire Pratt, I felt slightly better. I did not know her but her father, the poet E. J. Pratt, had been kind enough to tell me to keep writing when I was eighteen. If I had realized that she was an editor, I would have been awestruck. Since I did not know, she seemed simply a friend.

By now I was almost sorry we had come. We looked ridiculous. Not that anybody was looking at us. Jabber-jabber-jabber.

Then, all of a sudden, Mr McClelland and his satellites were there. They apologized and tried to fix things. Their ebullience made me believe that Margaret Laurence probably had been speaking of them when she had mentioned cocktails. They weren't drunk, but they certainly were in high spirits.

The Press refused to shift. They had started on their dinners. There were no other empty places.

Then waitresses came in with more dishes and glasses of tomato juice. Places were set especially for us at the end of each long table. I was hustled to my seat. Mother was led away. I could feel myself beginning to shake.

I glanced at the people seated on either side of me. Were they writers? Should I know them? I felt insignificant and as though I were not a prize-winning

twenty-nine-year-old, but a nobody of about twelve.
I gulped down my tomato juice and listened hard.

They were writers. They wrote things that went in
school textbooks. They talked to each other about
writing social studies for the junior high level. Once
a couple of them had muttered perfunctory greetings,
they ignored me. I had never been good at social
studies. I did not enjoy my dinner.

The program began. It went by me in a blur until
Margaret Laurence's turn came. She was asked to say
a few words. I felt sorry for her. But she recited an
African poem that left me moved and shaken. My few
words were nothing compared to that.

And how was I going to find my way to the stage?
I knew which end of the vast room it was at, but where
were the steps up to it? I had no idea. My tension
mounted.

I heard my name. I stood up, my knees shaking,
and stood there feeling lost. Then Claire Pratt took my
cold hand in her warm one.

"Your mother said you needed some help," she said
quietly. "Come with me."

I was on the stage. My few words whirled around
in my head. Mr McClelland was standing in front of
me — with my cheque held behind his back.

"Can you guarantee that the founder of Little, Brown
and Company is not an ancestor of yours?" he asked me.

"Yes . . . I think so," I stammered, ready to project
my three sentences of thanks.

"Then it gives me great pleasure to present you
with . . ."

The cheque was in my hand. I was smiling.

"Thank you," I said.

Two words were enough. I was led off the stage.

The long-awaited evening was over.

When I got back to my place, a reporter was waiting. Clutching my prize money, I tried to answer his quick questions.

"What did you do when you heard your first book was going to be published?" he asked.

"I shrieked with joy," I said truthfully. "Didn't you hear me in Toronto?"

The next day, in the Toronto *Star*, I read the headline with embarrassment.

AS AN AUTHOR SHE'S A SCREAMING SUCCESS.

Oh, well.

While Mother and I were driving home, I felt sad. Dad should have been there. If only he hadn't died eight years ago when I was twenty-one. He had helped me so much with my writing. He would have been so proud. My throat ached with missing him.

And I hadn't met any writers, not real writers. The whole evening, which was to have been so wonderful, had been instead a bitter disappointment.

Then I remembered the warm grin of the woman who had stood next to me, our backs to the wall. She wrote for adults and her book was about Africa. Even though I had never heard of her before, she was definitely a Canadian author. I would read this book of hers and I would not forget that she had made me welcome to the world of writers. She had seemed so pleased about my prize, too. I liked her even if she wasn't someone important.

I sighed and spoke my unworthy thoughts aloud. "I hope that Margaret Laurence turns out to be somebody," I said.

🏂 3 🏂

A Moment—We uncertain step
For newness of the night—
Emily Dickinson

I was tired. Whenever I turned my back, somebody hit somebody or somebody knocked something over or somebody whined, "Miss Little, do I *have* to do the *whole* page?" When my left eye began to hurt, it was the last straw.

"Janice Ferris, sit *still* and pay attention," I snapped. "Jimmy Boyd, leave Michael alone. Bryan, get to work. I want some peace and quiet in here."

The children stole sideways looks at each other and bent their heads over their arithmetic sheets. For two minutes there was not a sound. I knew it was too good to last. Sure enough, Bradley sent the tall container of wooden beads flying.

The small bright spheres and ovals rained down on the cement floor and went spinning in all directions. As they lodged under bookshelves, behind the guinea pig cage and under my desk, every one of my students gasped audibly and waited for me to explode. The clatter of the beads and the shocked, delighted, tensed stillness of the children were too much for me. I laughed.

Instantly, our usual bedlam was back.

I got down on my hands and knees and began retrieving the beads. Every child in the room tried to help.

"Keep going, Miss Little. There's one right in front of you," Alec said.

"No. To the left," Randy put in.

"Right, you mean," Alec told him.

As I did my best to follow these jumbled directions, I found my eye still hurting. It felt as though it had a grain of sand lodged under its lid. I rubbed at it, but that made the pain worse.

All the children who were ambulatory were chasing beads, scooping them up and carrying them to where I crouched, container in hand. We had retrieved most of them when Grant called, "The taxi's here. It's time to go home."

As I straightened and fetched Randy's wheelchair, Bryan came running up and held out the last bead.

"Thank you," I told the ring of expectant faces. They thought I could not manage without them — and they were right.

My eye was now watering badly. Once again I rubbed at it, even though I knew Mother would not approve.

"There's something in my eye," I said to Margaret. "But I can't seem to get it out, whatever it is. Do you think you. . ."

"No," Margaret said promptly and with extreme distaste. "I hate fiddling with somebody's eye. Why don't you go on home and let your doctor mother do it? I'll wait with the boys."

"You are a saint," I told her and sped to the phone.

Yet when we were home, and Mother had peered into my eye with her small magnifying glass, she could see no foreign object at all. She went to the telephone. "I'll call Bob Cowan. He won't mind. After all, he's right across the street."

Dr Cowan did not remove anything from my eye.

Instead, he kept peering into it with his slit lamp. Finally he told me I had a "bleb," something like a blister, on the surface of the cornea. He pricked it to relieve the pressure. He seemed concerned but did not discuss his findings. I went home, relieved that the pain had lessened, having no idea that that small bleb was only the beginning.

I was so happy that spring. Although it seemed a long time since the awards banquet, *Mine for Keeps* would be out in June. On the news I kept hearing about people digging fall-out shelters in their gardens. Maybe World War III really was imminent.

Dear God, I prayed, if there's going to be an atomic war, please keep it from happening till my book comes out.

I knew it was not a mature prayer. But the thought that the world might be blown to smithereens before I held that book in my hands was too terrible to contemplate.

I forgot the bleb. But two days later it happened again. And the day after that and three days later. Each time, my eye became a fiery red and was very painful. The only thing that gave me any relief was to have it bandaged tightly shut, so that it was immobilized. Margaret had to watch the kids for me while I returned to the doctor. When the condition did not clear up, Dr Cowan looked grave. He sent me to Toronto to see Dr Clement McCullough.

I braced myself. Even so, I was completely unprepared for Dr McCullough's diagnosis.

"Glaucoma," he said.

I stiffened, feeling cold and unreal. Grandma had had glaucoma. Her eye had had no sight, due to a cataract, and nobody had realized what had occurred until she had an acute attack of severe pain. She had been hospitalized immediately, and the afflicted eye had been removed. Was that going to happen to me?

Dr McCullough told me that mine was not that kind of glaucoma. My eye was not in immediate danger. I didn't ask for a prognosis. Mother would know.

He gave me drops to use daily.

"Will they cure it?" I did manage to ask.

He bent over the notes he was making.

"No," he muttered. "There isn't a cure. But if the blisters continue, we can operate."

The drops had no effect. The wretched blisters continued unabated. We arranged for me to have the operation in July. They would make a small opening through which the excess fluid in my eye could drain away, thus lowering the pressure on my cornea and putting an end to the blisters.

Well, at least my book would be out by then! Publication date was set for early in June. Friends were planning to give a big party to help me celebrate. I clung to the thought of it, putting off thinking about what would come afterward.

I wore an eye patch to immobilize my eye when it grew too painful, and I returned to the classroom. Teaching was difficult. Perhaps it was time for me to try writing full-time. My constant migraine headaches also pushed me in that direction. Before that June was over, I handed in my resignation.

Until the school year ended I taught doggedly on, and I waited for my complimentary copies of *Mine for Keeps* to arrive.

Just days before the publication date, the teamsters went on strike. My publisher told me sympathetically that the books had reached the border but could not be driven the rest of the way till the strike was settled. The celebration was called off. School finished. I said goodbye to the children. I did my best to do this cheerfully. When they followed my example, I was hurt.

When I checked into the Eye Wing of Toronto General Hospital, I had still not seen my precious first book. Dr McCullough, who was interested in my eyes but who seemed almost unaware of the rest of me, swept into my room trailed by a bevy of medical students. He talked to them in incomprehensible words, muttered a cursory greeting in my direction and swept out again. I had no idea what to expect. I did not even know whether I was going to have a local or a general anaesthetic. I was too overawed to ask. But my imagination, active at the best of times, told me that it would be far worse than the dentist's needles. Where would they put them in? The very thought made my toes curl.

Nevertheless, I behaved well that night. I joked with the nurses. When they left my room, I did not ring my bell. But I could not sleep. I was too obsessed by the unknown terrors ahead. I wanted my mother.

Before I was taken to the operating room the following morning, a nurse painted a large X on my forehead above my left eye. The need for this precaution did nothing to increase my confidence. I smiled wanly, waved to Mother and was wheeled away.

The needles were extremely unpleasant, and it was disconcerting to be able to see them coming. When they were over, I was alarmed to find that I could feel things happening to my eye. It was not particularly painful, but it was unnerving. Since the doctor had not once discussed the operation with me beforehand, I was certain I had not been given the correct amount of anaesthetic. I also imagined it was important that

I keep my eye absolutely still. This had never been easy for me, but I concentrated fiercely on managing it. Later one of the residents told me that not only was my eye completely immobilized by the anaesthetic, but the small tugs and pricks I felt during the surgery were perfectly normal.

"Some people sleep through the entire thing," he said.

As usual, I had transformed a not uncommon experience into an event of high drama.

After the first few hours of recovery, it was not my eye that gave me trouble; it was my back. I was instructed to lie perfectly still, flat on my back, and not stir. I could not sit up, roll onto my side, brush my hair or my teeth. I could not eat an apple. My acute back-ache was only one of the many in the Eye Wing. The nurses told me in bored voices that it would just last twenty-four hours. Then a kindly cleaning woman stopped long enough to fold a hand towel and slide it under the arch of my back. What a relief! If I had been allowed to sit up, I would have hugged her.

I made up my mind, then and there, always to be sympathetic with people suffering from chronic pain of any kind. Such a small thing as a folded towel could, I realized, often make such a difference. I would never be impatient or perfunctory again. It was a laudable resolve. I kept it — when I remembered.

Mother came as often as she could, but she had patients to look after, and my great-aunt Jen, now ninety-eight, needed care.

"I can't come tomorrow," she said on the second evening. "I have to do a day's work. But I'll be back the next afternoon."

The following morning I was feeling forlorn when a mysterious parcel was delivered to my room. The person who dropped it off whisked away to run further errands. I had no scissors. I started to tear it open with my teeth.

It felt like a book. I ripped off the last piece of paper and gasped.

It was *Mine for Keeps*.

4

By Chivalries as tiny,
A Blossom, or a Book,
The seeds of smiles are planted—
Which blossom in the dark.
                    Emily Dickinson

The previous summer, my sister Pat had been expecting her first child. One day Pat had said to me, "I've never loved babies the way you do. When they're old enough to start walking and talking, I like them. But those little ones make me nervous. What if, when this baby is born, I don't like it?"

"You'll feel differently when you see it," I had laughed. "If you don't, you can give it to me till it's bigger."

She had laughed, too, but I could tell she was still uneasy. I, who openly coveted all of my nephews and nieces, was startled. I hoped I was right about instant mother love.

When my new niece, Maggie, arrived, Mother took me to the hospital. We stopped to look at Maggie first. She was a comical-looking baby. Her hair stood straight up, as though her first sight of the world had alarmed her, and her small, pointy face had a knowing look. When we went into Pat's room, I said, "What a funny-looking daughter you have, with her hair all on end. Do you like her better than you thought you would?"

"She's not funny-looking," Pat said sharply. Then she added in a besotted voice, "She's beautiful. I loved her the minute I laid eyes on her. I think she's perfect."

Now, holding my first book, I knew exactly how she had felt. *Mine for Keeps* was beautiful, too. The cover picture glowed with warm summery colours. Sally looked exactly the way she should and so did Susie, her West Highland white terrier.

Like a new mother checking to make sure her baby has the regulation number of toes and fingers, I began examining my offspring and gloating over each fresh discovery.

I opened it somewhere in the middle, raised it to my face and took a great sniff. It smelled of paper, glue, ink and newness. It smelled just like my parents' books had long ago in Taiwan, like my first large print reader, like the shelves of beloved books in the Guelph Public Library and like my Complete Works of Shakespeare. The smell of a book is important to any reader, but of paramount importance to the reader who has to hold the book inches away from her nose before she can read it.

I turned back to the title page. Not only was my own name printed clearly upon it, but the page itself looked like a real title page.

I kept looking, turning the leaves with something close to reverence. My book had copyright information in it. It had contents. It had chapter headings.

Somehow I had missed the dedication. I backed up and found it.

To Dad

If only he were here! I had an instant picture of the broad smile he would be wearing as we studied each separate feature together. I had seen that grin when he saw my poems published, when he beheld an A on one of my essays in university, when he read a short story I had written. Not to be able to show him this miraculous first book brought an aching lump into my throat.

I blinked away the prickle of tears beginning and put through a call to Mother in Guelph.

"Dr Little's office," said Mother's receptionist.

"Hi, Mrs Maxey," I said. "Is Mother there?"

"No, Jean. She's at the hospital. How are you?"

"Fine," I said. What a stupid conversation! But I couldn't tell her about my book, not before I'd talked to Mother. "Could you ask her to call me when she comes in?"

"Is there any other message you'd like me to give her?" Mrs Maxey asked, detecting my suppressed excitement.

"No, thank you. Just have her call . . . as soon as she comes in."

I clutched my book and waited for the phone to ring or for someone, anyone, to enter my room. A nurse rustled in. Before I could say a word, she stuck a thermometer into my mouth. As she took my pulse, she looked everywhere but at my book. I waited. The minute the thermometer was withdrawn, I tried to tell her my news.

"I've just had a book published . . ." I started.

"That's nice, dear," she said, glancing at my book but not reaching for it. She gave an automatic smile and bustled off to the next patient.

I could not believe this. The most thrilling moment in my whole life had arrived and nobody was celebrating with me.

The phone!

I snatched up the receiver and half shouted, "Mother?"

"Yes," she said. "What's up?"

"*Mine for Keeps* . . . I have my first copy of *Mine for Keeps!*"

"Oh, Jean, how lovely," she said. "What does it look like?"

"I want you to come and see it," I told her. "I want you to come right now."

"And I want to come," she said, "but I'm afraid it just isn't possible this afternoon. I have a full line-up of appointments. I'll be there for sure tomorrow. It'll be just as beautiful then. I must go, dear. Someone is waiting. . . . See you tomorrow."

Click. She had hung up!

I removed the buzzing receiver from my ear and glared at it. Then I smacked it down hard on its cradle. I was tempted to pick the whole contraption up and hurl it at the wall.

Who was this someone waiting? One of the stupid patients, no doubt. All my life, whenever I needed my parents' attention, there had been some stupid patient waiting with a tale of woe. I called up the long procession of leaners, whiners, malingerers and hypochondriacs who had over the years gobbled up so much of my mother's free time. Why couldn't she put me first just once? Even now, stuck in a hospital, I didn't count as much as some stupid patient.

Ignoring the fact that Mother had been with me all day yesterday and was coming all the way to Toronto to be with me tomorrow, I wallowed in my misery.

"Sometimes I feel like a motherless child," I wailed at the unfeeling telephone, "a long way from home."

If only I had had the surgery in Guelph, there were lots of people . . .

I straightened up with a jerk. Elizabeth Pearson! She had been my friend ever since we had met when she was a camp director and I was a fifteen-year-old camper. She had shared other memorable moments in my life. When I had been certain I was going to fail my freshman year at university, she had wakened me with a long distance call to tell me that the examination results were in the morning paper and I had passed. She had also been the person Mother had called on that morning shortly after my twenty-first birthday when my father had died. Elizabeth had come to my college residence and broken the news and stayed with me while I packed to go home.

I dialed her number. She was there.

"I am sitting here in the hospital," I announced. Then I paused for effect. "With the very first published copy of *Mine for Keeps* in my hand!"

I waited for trumpets, wild cheers, a mighty peal of bells. Elizabeth did her best.

"How exciting," she said. "How does it look? Do you like it?"

"It's beautiful. It's perfect," I declared, sounding like Pat.

But telling her wasn't enough. I wanted to show it to her, to have her share my exultation. Aware that she, the mother of three small children, could not drop everything and fly to my side, I still hoped she would. I poured out my sad story. Mother could not come until tomorrow. The nurses and doctors didn't understand what a special day this was. I was supposed to be having a party and instead I was trapped in a big, heartless hospital.

When I ran out of complaints, she was sympathetic. She also sounded preoccupied. She had other things on her mind. Not stupid patients this time, I thought grimly. Stupid children.

"I know you're busy," I said, heaping on coals of fire, "but I just had to tell somebody."

"I'm glad you called," she said. "I'm coming, John. Wait."

Click. Grrr!

I looked through the book from cover to cover once again. Then, alone and friendless in a cruel world, I lay on my high bed with my first book clutched to my chest and gave way to what Georgette Heyer would call a fit of the dismals.

Ten minutes after Visiting Hours began, Elizabeth came flying in, laden down with gifts.

"I've got all three children waiting downstairs in the car," she panted, "but we can't let you not have a party."

As I watched, dumbfounded, she produced a chocolate cake with CONGRATULATIONS written across it. She also pulled out a package of balloons and, after blowing them up, she wrote felicitous words on them with a marking pen. HURRAH FOR THE AUTHOR! one read. Soon she had five of them stuck up around the window, on a picture and above the mirror. On a sausage-shaped one she printed PRIZE-WINNING BOOK!

The drab hospital room became filled with festivity and laughter. When a ward aide trotted in with a glass of juice, she stopped dead in her tracks.

"What's going on in here?" she demanded.

"It's a book launching party," Elizabeth told her, removing the juice glass and handing her *Mine for Keeps*. "This patient is a writer, you know, and this is her brand new very first book. Have some cake."

The bemused woman, still clutching my book in her left hand, accepted a square of cake in her right and downed it in three bites. Then she stood staring from me to the book and back again.

"I've never met a real, live author before," she breathed at last and scurried out the door to spread the news.

Having as yet no idea how much I would come to dislike that description of myself and my fellow writers, as though we ranked with the platypus or the koala bear, I felt excited and puffed-up with pride, exactly the way I thought an author should feel on Publication Day. That first sip of adulation is heady stuff. I beamed at the friend who had worked the miracle.

Elizabeth had snatched back the book before the aide disappeared with it. Now she sat down to look at it properly. Her open delight was exactly what I had been hungering for.

"It's gorgeous," she said. "Absolutely gorgeous. Your father would have been so proud."

Then she gave me a big hug and sped back to her children. I lay there and felt warmed right through. I did not yet know how rare are the people who can celebrate someone else's achievement so whole-heartedly.

From the moment Elizabeth departed, I was a celebrity. All and sundry now wanted to meet the real, live author. If they had not been told about my book before they entered my room, the rainbow balloons soon called their attention to it. Most of them had scant time for reading children's novels, but all of them were hungry for cake and, as they devoured the latter, they examined and exclaimed over the former.

"You're going home today," said the breezy nurse a few days later, poking her head in the door.

"Me?" I said blankly. "I thought Dr McCullough was away so I wasn't going till tomorrow. That's what they said at breakfast."

"I don't know about that," she said, "but I've been told to get this room ready. A judge needs it."

I felt indignant for a moment. Then I realized that, unexpected as this was, it meant I would soon be free. I called home. Mother could not come till after evening office hours. I called Elizabeth.

"Get your things packed," she said. "I'll be right over."

A friend in deed, that was Elizabeth Pearson.

"The Author" in the 1960s, with two friends.

⚡ 5 ⚡

Before I got my eye put out
I liked as well to See—
As other Creatures, that have Eyes
And know no other way—
          Emily Dickinson

I was hovering outside the door of the judge's room wait-ing for Elizabeth to pick me up when I saw a tall, stooped man in dark glasses tapping his way down the hall towards me. I backed up but, hearing me, he paused.

"What are you in for?" he asked in a melancholy voice.

"Glaucoma," I explained. "I was having blisters, but they've put in a hole to relieve the pressure. It'll be wonderful not having those blisters any longer."

"Hmph," he grunted. It was a disagreeable sound. I wished he would move on, but I could not bid him goodbye and go back into my room. His need to talk to someone held me there as inescapably as the Ancient Mariner's hand had detained the restive Wedding Guest.

"How about you?" I asked, doing my best to sound interested.

I was surprised when he let a moment of uncom-fortable silence fall between us. He was plainly agitated by his experience. Yet as I began to regret my question, his answer burst from him like an angry torrent push-ing away a dam.

"I have glaucoma, too," he said. "I had five operations which were supposed to fix everything. Now they've taken my eye out."

I shrank back, feeling as though an immense black shadow had loomed up in my path. Then, out of the corner of my eye, I glimpsed Elizabeth hurrying to my rescue. What did this elderly Jeremiah know about my prognosis? Nothing at all.

"My case is different," I said, turning away from him with relief. "I've got to go now. Goodbye."

As we went down the corridor, I tried to forget his raven's croak. My eye was different. I had never met anyone else with exactly the same problems.

But I couldn't forget. Five operations. Five. And then . . .

When, about a month later, my eye began to hurt, I heard his angry voice inside my head, repeating the unbelievable words. Mother was in her office. I knocked.

"Come in here," she said, "where there's a good light."

I waited, my heart leaden. I heard her catch her breath.

"I'm afraid it is a blister," she said, sounding sick.

The next morning, Dr Cowan peered at my cornea and sighed. The tiny opening Dr McCullough had made to relieve the pressure had become blocked by floating debris. Back in Toronto, I listened while Dr McCullough explained that one layer of my iris was unravelling. He used other words, but I had this picture of bits of it coming loose and causing trouble.

"We can try again, this time putting in a wick that should keep the opening clear," he said, sounding morose.

"You're the one who knows," I said. "We'll do what you say."

The second operation was less traumatic. This time I knew what was coming. I still did not, however, drift off to sleep.

The wick was not effective, either. I think it slipped. The blebs began to form once more. I had a third operation. A doughnut-shaped wick was tried instead of one shaped like a spatula. It, too, failed, and the blisters returned.

Mother and I sat in Dr McCullough's office again. I kept wanting to cry but just managed not to.

"My colleague thinks we should try again," the doctor said in his dry, distant voice. "But I think you would be foolish to take that route. I would advise you to have the eye enucleated."

Enucleated? I looked at Mother. She cleared her throat. Her voice sounded dry, too, as she translated for me.

"Enucleation means having the eye removed."

A tag end of poetry surfaced in my brain. Emily Dickinson's. I concentrated on it for an instant, giving myself time.

> Before I got my eye put out
> I liked as well to See —
> As other Creatures . . .

Dr McCullough's gruff voice snapped me out of my trance.

"You can have that done in Guelph, of course," he said. "I'll be in touch with your doctor there."

The visit was over. I swallowed and started getting ready to stand up and walk out the door.

The doctor was not at his best with people. Perhaps he knew this. He said defensively, "We are learning more all the time. If you had come in here ten years ago, we couldn't have done anything for you."

Maybe he did not fully understand how little real use my left eye was to me. I, however, thought of the stressful twelve months I had just lived through and wished I had come earlier and no operations had been attempted.

As Mother and I picked up our purses and rose to go, he added one last shattering sentence. He turned his back before he said it. He may have thought we were already out of earshot.

"When glaucoma develops in the other eye, perhaps we will have learned the way to save it."

Neither of us answered. I kept my face stiff. I knew I should ask him to repeat himself, but I could not get the words to come out. Mother thanked him and we left. As we walked down the hall, I said without looking at her, "Did you hear what he said?"

"I heard," she said.

"Did he mean . . ." I could not finish.

My mother said, "Jean, don't start stewing about what may happen some day. Even Dr McCullough can't read the future."

She did her best to sound calm, but I knew from her voice that she was almost as shocked as I.

I did try not to think ahead. After all, I was going to have my left eye out. Worrying about what might be lying in wait for my right eye seemed premature. I had a present bridge to get across. It was a long, covered bridge. Approaching the tunnel entrance, I saw nothing but darkness. Once I entered that darkness, it would be awhile before I would glimpse the light again, let alone know for certain that I would emerge. Night might even fall before I got that far.

I reminded myself that enucleation would put paid to those blisters. I also kept peering into the dense fog which was all my left eye now discerned. I could distinguish light from dark, was aware of a blur of green when I stared at a grassy field, watched it change to a blur of white when I turned to look at the dusty road. I could no longer see curbs, recognize people, count my own fingers. The eye was useless. Getting rid of it was a good idea.

The many people who assured me that nobody would ever know my plastic eye from a real one were no comfort. "We have a man on our staff with one, and until I was told, I didn't notice it at all."

Not one of them seemed to realize that they had just informed me that if I myself did not tell people one of my eyes was a fake, somebody else would be sure to do it for me.

As the day for the operation neared, I began to feel unreal. I could not understand why but I grew more and more afraid. And, as much as I flinched from the thought of everything that went with eye surgery, what I really feared was something quite different, something that I found hard to explain. I, who had been cross-eyed since birth, was convinced that the removal of my eye and the substitution of a prosthetic one would somehow turn me into a stranger. An imposter maybe. A freak.

I had read several articles about how deeply disturbed servicemen were by an accident that radically interfered with their body image. I had thought this a bit silly. What did it matter that they had to come home minus a leg? Oh, I sympathized with their problems in adapting to a disability. But those who loved them would go on caring despite the alteration in their outward appearance. And the others scarcely mattered. These men were making a big fuss over nothing.

Now I found their dread taking hold in my own heart. I had been cross-eyed all my life. That misshapen, eccentric, too small eye was part of my psyche, part of me. Without it, I might look more "normal," but who would I be? Not Jean Little.

When I tried to talk about this, my friends laughed.

"You'll still be yourself," they said, secure in their own familiar, whole bodies. "It won't make any difference at all."

I thought about all the people I knew who had had to get false teeth. Did they feel this strangeness? Probably. Had I laughed at them? I was sure I had.

I did my best to joke about my upcoming ordeal, of course. The jests were hollow, but I had my reputation to maintain. Everyone knew I was well adjusted, light-hearted, quick with a quip.

"You have such a great sense of humour," they insisted.

At this point, I had never knowingly seen such a thing as an artificial eye. I, along with most people, had a hazy idea that they were made of glass, were incapable of moving in a normal manner and were spherical in shape. I was wrong on all counts.

Dr Cowan now explained to me, "When your blind eye is removed, a plastic ball will be inserted in the eye socket in such a way that the muscles that move the real eye will move the plastic ball instead. Since this ball will be held in place by muscles, you won't be able to take it out any more than you can take your real eye out now. When your eye socket has had a chance to heal, you will go to Toronto and be fitted for a prosthetic eye. You'll be able to take it out easily to clean it or to have it polished. It looks like a shell, I guess. It'll fit over the ball and be kept in place by your upper and lower lids."

"Is it something like a giant contact lens?" I asked, more fascinated than repelled.

"Well . . . a little, I suppose. You'll understand it much better once you've seen one. These artificial eyes are so skilfully made that they appear perfectly normal. The plastic ball moves the prosthesis so that it seems to glance from side to side in a way that's truly life-like. It's uncanny."

Dr Cowan told me most of this before I had the surgery, but it all sounded implausible. As I was being wheeled into the operating room, he told me my first plastic eye joke. It was all about a naval officer who had a Union Jack painted on a spare eye and, when everyone was getting a bit tipsy, slipped it in instead of his real prosthesis. Other officers would take one look and refuse another drink. It helped us over an emotionally charged couple of minutes.

When I came to, Mother was there. I just had time to smile at her and notice my throat hurt before I began throwing up. Nobody had warned me that my body would strenuously object to having a plastic ball permanently inserted.

After forty-eight hours of acute misery, my body gave in and let the plastic ball stay. Mother was with me most of that time. Without her there, it would have been hard to bear. As a matter of fact, I thought it unbearable even with her beside me.

When the bad time was over and I could listen,

Mother read aloud to me for hours on end. I half listened. I was tired and my life seemed in abeyance. When she began a new novel by Elizabeth Goudge, I was pleased until I discovered that the hero was a blind writer. His life seemed ridiculously idealized to me. The one thing I envied him was his marvellous guide dog, Bess.

"I'd like a dog like that," I said listlessly. "Having such a beautifully trained dog would be one good thing about going blind."

Books about blind people always talked about them living in darkness, endless night. Yet even with the bandages in place, I was aware of a brownish-charcoal with shifting bits of colour.

The doctors gathered. Scissors snipped. Tape pulled at my eyebrow and then came loose. Then, with my right eye, I saw that they were peering into my left socket with a small bright flashlight. I switched over to look out my left eye.

It was unsettling, unreal. Yet it was interesting, too. I saw not blackness but a dull brownish background with vivid bits of colour that moved and changed as I watched. There were green pin pricks that swelled into blue circles, streamers of pink, all scurrying around, fading and flowering, flowing and shrinking, skimming off sideways and disappearing while something else swam into sight.

I was to find that, even in the dead of night, when all my right eye could see was blackness, my left remained less black and, if I waited, the kaleidoscopic colours would begin their fireworks.

"You're doing fine," one of the doctors said, remembering all at once that this eye socket was part of a human being.

"I'm glad," I said, trying to mesmerize myself with the glowing splashes of colour. I had to concentrate to keep myself from the realization that, for the first time in my life, a bright light was shining directly into my eye and I could not see it.

I said nothing. My usual ready flow of chat had dried up. The doctors went out, talking in overly hearty voices.

I turned to where I knew Mother was.

"How did it look?" I said brightly. "Did you see?"

"Like a wound," she said. She did not feel chatty, either.

"I think I'll sleep awhile," I said and shut my eyes.

As the doctors had walked out, a familiar part of me seemed to have departed with them. I was not sure how important that part was, but I felt sure that it was irretrievably lost.

The tears seeping out from under my closed lids did not notice that only one eye was real.

6

It's all I have to bring today—
This, and my heart beside—
This, and my heart, and all the fields—
And all the meadows wide—
                    Emily Dickinson

The NO VISITORS sign was taken off my door. Friends came to see me. Relatives arrived. I was showered with flowers and candy and determined good cheer.

"Where did you get that black eye?" everyone and his aunt asked. "Who gave you the shiner? How does the other fellow look?"

They were teasing, relaxed. But their eyes shifted quickly.

I did my best to respond in kind. After all, they were so much better than the weepers, the ones who hung onto my hand and murmured mournfully, "Poor dear. I know, I know. You've had more than your share of troubles."

Still, I wished they would all stay away. Pretending everything was fine was almost beyond me. And some of them stayed so long!

Before the first day was over, I felt a high wall go up between myself and my "normal" friends. It was a wall of glass. I could see through it. I could hear voices. But it changed the world from a real place where there were scents, a multitude of voices, laughter, singing, the touching of hands, to a world where all of these common things were remote.

One day, after many people had dropped in, I lay weeping, wishing something would be ordinary, longing to feel like myself, to be the person I had been before the blisters began.

Margery MacKay, a dear, gentle, humorous friend, came in with a small bouquet when Visiting Hours had only three minutes to go. She smiled, said something kind and slipped away, leaving the vase of flowers on the table that swung across my bed. I sat up, my face wet with tears, and lifted the vase to where I could see the one rose surrounded by sweetpeas. Their fragrance reached me before I could see their soft tints. They spoke of a world still bright, still lovely, waiting for me to get well and return to it.

Although I was so exhausted that I could not stop crying, I felt hope touch me. Maybe, after awhile, I would again be Jean Little and not this isolated stranger. Maybe.

Then I felt strong enough to try reading. I took up a book. It was one that had been recommended to me by a Guelph librarian. It was the first volume of a trilogy. I had not started it because, when I had glanced inside it casually, it had seemed to be about elves.

The Fellowship of the Ring by J. R. R. Tolkien, I read. Ready to be won over by good writing, I flipped to the first page. I focussed my eye on the opening sentence and discovered, with a sick horror, that my eye would not stay focussed there. It jerked halfway down the page, flitted back to the third or fourth line, skidded across a paragraph . . .

Mother came in, took one look at me and stopped in her tracks.

"What's wrong?" she said.

"I can't read," I got out. "My eye won't stay on the line."

"I'm sure it's a temporary thing," she said. "After all, think what an adjustment your eye is having to make. Rest it now and I'll read to you. Do you want me to read that book?"

"No." I thrust the elf story aside. How was I to guess that it was the very book that might have given me both escape and new courage? She read something else. But I did not hear much of whatever it was. What if this was not temporary? What if, from this day forward, I would be unable to read or write?

Although I had had considerable nystagmus before the operation, I had learned to read in spite of it. Until this minute, it had only given me trouble when I was overtired.

Temporary. Temporary.

Dr Cowan was unconcerned. "Give yourself time," he said. "It has some adjusting to do. Stress does funny things. Listen to the radio for awhile. You don't have to start reading immediately."

He might not have needed to read right away, but reading was central in my life. If I couldn't read. . . . The dread that had haunted me before Margery came returned tenfold. Life deprived of books was not life at all.

I went home. I was not to get my plastic eye for a month. A piece of clear plastic, shaped to resemble the eye but perforated, was put in its place during those first weeks.

I was grateful for this time alone. I did not want to see anyone. I rejected eye patches.

"They make you look like a pirate," Mother said.

"I don't want to look like a pirate," I growled.

"But if you go out . . ." At my fierce look, she left the sentence hanging.

"I'm not going anywhere," I said through shut teeth.

I was a wounded animal and I wanted to hide. I needed to be solitary, to explore the extent of my hurt in private. Except for Mother, I did not want to be with well people.

All I thought about was my hunger for books, my need to read.

Grimly, I made up my mind to control my disobedient eye. What I needed was a book with strong, very black, clear print. I would force my eye to follow each line until it remembered what to do.

I knew, without having to look through the hundreds of books that lined the floor-to-ceiling shelves in my bedroom, which books were perfect. Rosemary Sutcliff's novels for young people had exactly the strong, black type I required. I owned a whole row of them. I remembered reading *Warrior Scarlet* to the kids at the Centre. It was still my favourite, I thought, but I could not bear to read it now. Drem's struggle to learn to live with one arm he could not use would cut too close to the bone.

Ignoring *Warrior Scarlet*, I stooped to scan the row of Sutcliff books. Then, without asking myself why, I reached for my worn copy of *Outcast*. That single bleak word seemed to call me. It fitted me better than my name.

It was mid-afternoon. Sunlight spilled in through the window. Unaware of its warm light, I settled down on my bed and turned on the extra brightness of my electric light so that every word stood out in as sharp a contrast as possible. Susie, my small, shaggy West Highland terrier, jumped onto the bed and snuggled against me. I did not notice. I began to drag my eye along the lines of print. It worked. It did not take all that long for my eye to recover its old skimming ability.

I did not put down the book, though. By the end of the first chapter, I had forgotten my poor vision. I was Beric, the child snatched from the sea and not really belonging. He and I were sold into slavery. As I pulled the heavy oar with him, I, too, came to care for the man who rowed beside me in the Roman galley and, finally, I came back to Britain and found my home and my freedom.

I read the whole book the way a traveller in the desert gulps down a long drink of lifesaving water. When I closed it, I knew I had not lost my world after all. My cheeks felt stiff, scoured with tears. It was almost suppertime. I turned off the lamp and stood looking out into the darkening sky. Then I saw my first star since I had gone into the hospital.

I knew it was unaware of human existence, and yet it seemed to be sending me a private and particular blessing. I stood smiling back at it for a moment. Rosemary Sutcliff had made me weep and, unlike the tears of exhaustion I had cried the afternoon Margery came, these, shed not for my pain but for Beric's, had unlocked the door of the grey prison in which I had been living in solitary confinement for days.

Reached by a story, touched by a star, I was not a stranger to myself any longer.

♯ 7 ♯

A Letter is a joy of Earth—
It is denied the Gods—
        Emily Dickinson

I felt queasy as we rode the elevator up to the office of Le Grande Optical. I was wearing a detestable eye patch and, whatever Mother said, I was not feeling piratical.

"Jean Little next." Mother and I followed the speaker.

"If you'll sit here," he said, guiding me to a chair that he could raise and tip back with his toe. Settling myself in it, I wondered if it had been intended for a barber or a dentist. Or did plastic eye fitters have their own brand? I was relieved that it didn't tip as far back as the dentist's. I felt vulnerable enough without being turned practically upside-down.

Then the man looked at my right eye and said casually, "Let's see. Your eyes are brown."

Brown! I was struck dumb with shock. Ever since I could remember, I had been told my eyes were blue like Dad's. I had bought clothes that "brought out the blue" in them. Had everyone lied? My eyes were blue, blue, blue.

He must not have looked properly.

"No! Blue," I blurted, waiting for confirmation from my mother. "My eyes are blue."

He leaned forward and peered at them. Mother said not a word.

"Well, not really blue," the man said in a kindly tone such as one uses when addressing a small, silly child. "Grey, perhaps. Definitely not blue."

"Mother, they are blue, aren't they?" I demanded.

"Well, a blue-grey," she said. "Maybe more grey."

I had imagined I was getting one new eye today. Now both were changing. While I tried to rearrange my picture of myself, the man pulled out a drawer full of eyes.

When I went to Toronto in 1987 to get a new prosthetic eye, they first made a mould of my eye socket and then custom-made the prosthesis. The iris was hand-painted so that the colour exactly matched my good eye. It took the technician most of the day to make it. But in 1963, buying a plastic eye was much more like shopping for shoes. You chose from the stock available.

The eye man picked one and slipped it in. It felt strange.

"Too big," he muttered, removing it deftly and turning to contemplate his other choices.

Astonished as I was by the idea of all those many eyes looking up at him, I tried to concentrate. I had a request I had prepared for this very moment.

"Could you make an eye that would look like my real one?" I asked before he could insert his next selection. "Then I would still look like myself. And they would match. That's what I want."

He glanced at the eye in question and shook his head.

"No," he told me firmly. "You don't want an eye that looks abnormal. From now on, people will think the artificial eye is the real one. It is much better that way. You'll see."

He spoke with such conviction that I, who had no experience to go on, subsided. He slid in a second eye. When I blinked, it swivelled around loosely. Mother, who had moved over to where she could look on, actually laughed.

"I'm sorry, but you do look so funny," she excused herself. "Cock-eyed, I guess you'd say."

I was furious. This was no laughing matter. I did not say a word, though, partly because I was so mad and partly because saying one word would have started me crying.

"Too small," the expert muttered, popping it out. "And too dark, I think."

At last he had one that fit. Mother stepped forward to see.

"It looks so natural," she marvelled. "Really, Jean, nobody would ever know it was plastic. It's amazing. Absolutely amazing."

I felt confused and angry. So what if my right eye was smaller than a normal one and was so scarred that no pupil was visible. I could see with it, couldn't I? I resented the way they dismissed it in favour of a piece of painted plastic which, for all its natural appearance, saw not one thing. It was purely cosmetic and a fraud.

As the man told me how to care for my new body part, I listened in grim silence. Once we were in the car, I tried to explain my muddled feelings to Mother and ended up in tears.

"Well, at least the fake eye cries just as well as the real one," I gulped, trying to resurrect my famous sense of humour.

"I've noticed," said my mother.

I soon found out, though, that the man had been right in refusing to give me an eye that looked like my old one. People always gazed into that fake eye. Even my friends and relations, although they knew perfectly well it was just a piece of plastic, forgot and smiled into it. If they were sitting close to me on a couch, they seemed to stare right past me. It was unnerving.

Despite my initial resentment, by the time we got home that day, I had begun to feel slightly more cheerful. After all, I now had this new eye. Once I grew used to it, I could get on with my writing. I knew that nothing would be as healing as turning on my brand-new electric typewriter and escaping into the world of my story.

I was thinking about this as we sat down to a late lunch.

"Jean," Mother said suddenly, her voice filled with wonder, "your eyes move together now!"

"What?" I said, staring at her, not quite understanding.

"You are looking straight at me with both eyes right this minute," she said. "Your left eye is not sliding sideways. "You . . ."

But I was no longer there. I ran to the mirror in the front hall to see for myself. There was a bright light above that mirror, and I could get close to it. I stared at myself.

And both my eyes were looking back. Not only that, but my left eye looked exactly like anybody else's. Until that moment, even though I had been told my eyes were abnormally small and my pupils almost invisible, the eyes I saw were simply my eyes. I did not compare them to others, not when it came to size.

But now I had an eye with a pupil I could see for myself, an eye much bigger than the one I had lost. A real eye.

It isn't, I reminded myself, but I was smiling at my own image. And my new eye smiled back at me. I was not cross-eyed!

I turned to grin at Mother who had followed me. Then I switched eyes. The instant I did so, I myself felt my unused right eye slide over to the left. If I remembered always to use my seeing eye, my strabismus would no longer be evident. If I forgot . . .

As we finished lunch, I felt buoyant. I felt as though I had been newly created. And I felt a pang of disloyalty. My discarded left eye had, after all, been able to see.

It had never been my "good" eye. It had only had 12/400ths visual acuity even in the pre-glaucoma days. I had been able to read only headlines with it, and of late these, too, had blurred.

I did try to remember not to switch eyes but, when my right eye grew tired or I was bored, I would sit staring into nothingness, giving no thought to what my eyes were up to. At such times I almost always changed over. It was so restful.

Knowing that I could look people, strangers especially, more or less straight in the eye increased my self-confidence immensely. Becoming a published writer helped enormously also. No longer did I mumble, "I write." I spoke instead of my first book and my editor in Boston.

When I had to fill in "Occupation" on a form, though, I still wrote "Teacher." Putting down "Writer" seemed too brazen.

Yet it was high time I got on with book number two.

I feared that beginning a second book when the first had won an award would prove a totally different experience from feverishly writing a first novel. It seemed frightening until I wrote the first five sentences. I discovered, much to my own relief, that the minute I moved inside Jenny Macgregor's head, I left Jean Little behind. Even when I reached the bottom of the first manuscript page, rolled it out of my typewriter and held it up close to my working eye so I could read it over, even when I realized that it was not good enough and began again, even when I eventually had a first draft of the first chapter and started on Chapter Two, I was too intent on Jenny's grief over the death of her twin brother to back off and look at my work with the eyes of a critic.

Not once did I stop to ask myself what reading level I was writing for; not once did I wonder whether teachers, librarians and parents would buy a book in which a family was grieving over the death of a child; not once did I realize that I was writing a Problem Novel. I simply wrote and rewrote and re-rewrote Jenny and Mike's story, let them shape their own lives and, over and over again, was surprised and delighted by the unexpected things they said and did.

I did, however, hold on to one resolution. I decided to use my story to express my gratitude to Rosemary Sutcliff for rescuing me from my "evening of the mind."

Jenny's father was a librarian. After his son Michael's funeral, he read Rosemary's novels aloud to his daughter. One paragraph ended:

> . . . And as Jenny shared the heartbreak and loneliness of Beric, Tamsyn, Drem and the rest, her own heartache was eased and she began to share in the beauty and the hope in the stories — the colors of flowers she had never seen, the spring weather, the love of animals, the inner light of kindness.

It was the best way I could think of to tell the renowned author what her books had meant to me personally and to alert children who had not yet discovered her stories to their power.

I mailed in the manuscript with trepidation. Now that it was done, I did remember that it was just my second book. What if my editor, Miss Jones, wrote, "Nice try, but I'm afraid we can't use it. It falls so far short of the talent you seemed to show in *Mine for Keeps*."

I had often read reviews that began, "Although John Smith's second novel shows some talent, it is a crashing disappointment to those of us who recall his powerful and innovative first book . . ."

When Miss Jones' letter reached me, I ripped it open with hands that shook. The first sentence jigged about so that I could not read a word. Then at last I deciphered the incredible opening sentence.

Congratulations on a beautifully disciplined piece of writing!

I stared at the words in shock. Nobody had ever called anything of mine "beautifully disciplined." I seriously considered having the letter framed and hung in a prominent place where my family would be sure to see it daily.

When, a year or so later, the first complimentary copies of *Home from Far* reached me, I sent one, along with a copy of *Mine for Keeps*, to Rosemary Sutcliff care of her publisher.

I had no idea that she had been disabled since early childhood with Still's Disease, a form of arthritis that affects young children. I simply could not resist sending her my entire body of work. All two of them.

Obeying post office regulations, I did not enclose my letter telling her what reading *Outcast* had meant to me. I taped it onto the outside of the package instead, putting the right number of stamps on both parcel and letter. "Don't bother replying," I said, but I headed my epistle with my address.

May was half over when, sorting through the mail, I came upon a blue airmail form from Britain. I slit it open with a paper knife so that I would not accidentally destroy something vital. It was hard to do because, once again, my hands were shaking.

> *Dear Jean Little,*
> *What a lovely surprise! I took both books to bed with me, and neglected all the work I had meant to take, and read one one evening and the other the next. Was so thrilled to find the mention of my books in "Home from Far," which I loved, but "Mine for Keeps" I think I loved even more. You have done Sal so beautifully. . . . You must remember your own childhood very well. Oh, how you make me remember . . .*
> *I shall treasure both books. Thank you again for sending them to me.*
>
> *Yours,*
> *Rosemary Sutcliff*

Rosemary Sutcliff loved my books! And she understood what I had been trying to say in Sal's story.

Yet I saw right away that she had not received my letter. She clearly had no notion why the books had been sent to her.

I should write back. After all, she must be curious.

Another blue airmail form came almost by return mail. Its kindness was such that I wrote a third letter telling her that I was going to be in England in June.

Was there any possibility that we might meet? If she were in the middle of writing a book I would, of course, not dream of interrupting her. But if she happened to be between books . . .

By now I knew about the uneasy time that comes when one book is done and the idea for the next has not yet presented itself.

We were leaving Canada before word from Rosemary could reach Guelph. I sent her a list of the hotels where we would be staying. I explained that once I arrived in England, I would be visiting my aunt Dorothy in Buckinghamshire but that I and my "guide person" friend Carol Johnston would be pleased to travel to Sussex if Rosemary had time to spare.

Her postcard caught up with us in Florence.

> *Come to lunch and stay to tea. We'll have Spiller's Shapes for your friend. Does she wear a harness and sit before crossing the road?*

It took me a moment to figure out that Spiller's Shapes must be a British dog biscuit.

🐾 8 🐾

I never saw a Moor—
I never saw the Sea—
Yet know I how the Heather looks
And what a Billow be
Emily Dickinson

Carol and I were on the train on our way to Barnham Junction. I clutched my purse with Rosemary's last letter and card inside it. I didn't get them out and reread them. I knew their contents by heart.

I stared at Carol. She was writing her brother a letter. How could she be so calm? We had first met at a summer camp a year before, and we had found ourselves friends from the first. I had not guessed until now how insensitive she was. Imagine coolly catching up on her correspondence at a time like this.

I did not know that she was scribbling,

> *We are on our way to meet a famous writer who is a friend of Jean's. . . . We are slightly apprehensive, to say the least!*

Carol glanced at her watch, put away her letter and started looking out the window for our stop.

"This is it," she said. "Come on."

Rosemary's father was there to meet us — a tall, shy man who, as we drove to Walberton, increased my anxiety by telling me that Rosemary had visitors from all over the world.

Important visitors. Witty, interesting, special visitors.

Then it gradually dawned on me that he was like my father. He thought his daughter was the most gifted person alive. Captain Sutcliff was not obliquely informing me that my coming to visit Rosemary was presumptuous; he was simply celebrating the fact that yet another visitor, myself, thought it important to make a long journey to meet the person he loved best.

I relaxed a trifle. Then I remembered the problem of whether or not to shake hands. Only those with limited vision can appreciate the complications of shaking hands with someone you cannot see clearly. I had learned always to extend my hand first. Then the sighted person had to take it and I would not need to fumble. But Rosemary Sutcliff was handicapped. What if I held out my hand where she couldn't reach it? What if hers was painful?

I had not yet realized that you pay a price for the "gift" of an active imagination. While mine played a major part in making me a writer, it also made me adept at transforming run-of-the-mill molehills into towering mountain ranges.

Rosemary's father showed us into a gracious living-room with big windows at both ends and departed.

Then Carol proved her worth.

"There are your books," she whispered, pointing to the pair of them standing side by side in book-lined shelves.

Instantly, I felt almost at home. Rosemary already knew me, after all, and I knew her, too. We had lived inside each other's novels. That was the best way to meet another writer.

We spoke in whispers.

"What's a tenterhook?" I hissed.

"I haven't the slightest idea," Carol breathed, choking back laughter born of sheer nervousness.

Then Captain Sutcliff came back and led us into Rosemary's workroom.

There she was, a small, polite, faceless person sitting behind a table. For one moment, which felt to me like a couple of hours, I was tongue-tied. Then, as we exchanged greetings, I began to babble. I could hear myself doing it, but I could not stop. What threw me off balance was hearing Rosemary's English accent. I ought to have expected this, of course, but her letters had sounded only slightly British, and her books had no alien accent at all.

We talked about accents. We talked about the weather. We talked about a whole list of inconsequential

Rosemary.

things. It was not the way I had hoped it would be. We were all far too polite. But I did not know what to do about it.

The moment that broke the ice came after lunch when we moved out into the sunny walled garden.

My head had started to ache long before we reached Burnham Junction. By now the pain was ferocious. I was not surprised. Tension and migraine headaches had been part of my life since childhood.

I reached into my purse for pills. Rosemary was concerned.

"Perhaps you shouldn't be sitting in the sun," she said.

"Oh, my mother says it's just tension," I said lightly.

I swallowed two capsules, leaned forward to set down the tumbler and settled back into the lawn chair. There was an ominous ripping noise. The next thing I knew, the canvas back of the chair had separated from the wooden seat, and I had plummeted down into the framework that remained.

I had broken my hostess's furniture. She was, of course, appalled. Carol, my insensitive friend, was helpless with laughter. And I was not only embarrassed; I was stuck!

I struggled to emerge with dignity, but there was no hope. When I tried to lever myself up and out frontwards, splinters jabbed into me and pinned me down.

"Carol, stop laughing!" I growled.

She didn't. Perhaps she tried, but one glance at me set her off again. In the end I got free by wriggling out of the chair backwards. All formality was at an end forever.

When I, bruised and with a large tear in the back

of my dress, was seated in a whole chair, we really began talking.

"I've finished the first draft of a new book," I told Rosemary. "It's a sequel to *Mine for Keeps* but the main character isn't Sally but her younger sister. My sister Pat said to me, "You've written about how hard it is to be a handicapped child. Now you should write about how hard it is to be the sister of someone who is handicapped.""

We laughed. Then I went on. "At the beginning, Meg's mother promises her a room of her own. Then the grandmother comes to live with them and Meg's mother has to break that promise. Just before I left, I got a letter from Miss Jones telling me that they think I must change it. A mother mustn't go back on her word apparently."

Rosemary snorted.

"The woman must live in a cloud cuckooland," she said. "*All* mothers have to break promises occasionally. Stick to your guns. It's your story."

I stared at her in delighted disbelief. I had never before spoken with a writer this way. Miss Jones, with her crisp voice of authority, overawed me. I feared to argue lest Little, Brown would decide my books weren't really worth publishing.

It was heady to hear a great children's writer dismiss an editor's dictum with such scorn. I learned in that instant that while editors had their uses, they were not infallible. I should occasionally fight back.

"Now that I've written a book about a crippled child," I told her, "people keep urging me to write about a deaf kid or one with cystic fibrosis. I can't and I can't explain why not."

"You write the book that comes to you asking to be

written," Rosemary said. "Books aren't made to order, not good ones."

She gave me the strength to resist the many suggestions I was to get over the years. From then on I stood firm except when the book itself marched into my head and made me write it.

Carol and I said goodbye. Back in our London hotel, I wept tears of self-pity because the magical day towards which I had been living for so long was suddenly over, and I had not said any of the deeply significant things I had dreamed of saying.

And why couldn't I have tried listening for once?

"I talked too much," I wailed.

"Never mind," said Carol.

In Canada again, I sent my dress to be invisibly mended, wrote Rosemary a thank-you letter and got back to work on my manuscript. I felt very alone. Why didn't Rosemary live in Guelph? Maybe if I lived in Toronto I'd get to know other writers.

Still, Rosemary's letters brought her nearer to me than my next-door neighbours. A few years later, I learned that while my favourite book during my childhood had been *The Secret Garden*, one of Rosemary's had been L. M. Montgomery's *Emily of New Moon*. Discovering this delighted me. There we had been, two little girls in love with stories, Rosemary living blissfully for awhile in Prince Edward Island while I, with equal joy, moved to Yorkshire. Who needed a magic carpet?

9

I dwell in Possibility—
A fairer House than Prose—
More numerous of Windows—
Superior — for Doors—

Of Chambers as the Cedars—
Impregnable of Eye—
And for an Everlasting Roof
The Gambrels of the Sky—

Of Visitors — the fairest—
For Occupation — This—
The spreading wide my narrow Hands
To gather Paradise—
            Emily Dickinson

The next summer I sat on the dock at a family friend's cottage, gazing out over Lake Rosseau.

Mother's voice broke in on my reverie. "Agnes mentioned that Miss Cowan, whose cottage is just around the bay, knew my brother Gordon. We're going over to see her. Do you want to come along?"

"Sure," I said, though I was feeling almost too lazy to move.

As we neared the cottage in question, we saw a small boy, about four years old, run up to an elderly woman who was picking wildflowers.

"Look at this one," he cried, holding out a speckled stone he had found. "See how it sparkles."

"Yes," she said smiling. "But see. We have visitors."

He ducked behind her as we came up and were introduced. Miss Cowan had been a schoolteacher, it transpired. Uncle Gordon, Mother's oldest brother who had been killed in World War I, had been a student of hers. He had given her his swagger stick before going overseas. She still had it. As I sat listening to Mother and Miss Cowan talk about years gone by, her great-nephew became brave enough to venture out on his explorations again. Every so often he would trot up with some treasure to show her — a flower, a caterpillar, another stone. She accepted each new offering with great interest and took time to tell him the names of the flowers.

She told us she had designed the cottage and had it built to her own specifications. She said that she was in the habit of inviting a great-niece or nephew to visit her. She entertained them one at a time and it gave each a chance to have somebody's entire attention for awhile. Watching these two, you could see how joyously they shared in exploring and reading and simply being together.

The instant we were out of earshot, I turned to my mother.

"I want a cottage," I announced. "The others all have their own homes. It's time I got a place, too. I could have the kids come to visit one by one, the way she does. That would be so much fun. I could get to know them individually."

Mother plainly thought I was crazy but, as always, she listened. Over the years she had had to give ear to countless sudden and usually passing enthusiasms of mine.

But the next weekend my brother Jamie and his wife

and kids came for a visit. I soon persuaded them to drive me around to look at the two or three properties up for sale close to Guelph. Nothing we saw resembled the place of my dreams. Mother was relieved when we came back and reported our failure.

She relaxed too soon. The next Saturday I looked in the Properties for Sale section of the newspaper.

"It can't hurt to go and see," I told her. "We could think about it better if we knew what was available."

There was a cottage near Bala. There was another not too far to take in on the same trip. And there was a third ad that fascinated me.

Point of land with small private island.
700' of shoreline. Call Utterson.

It wouldn't do for us, of course. We needed property with a cottage already built. But imagine owning a tiny island . . .

Mother sighed and took me north. The first place had a square little lawn, a flagstone path, neat flowerbeds and awnings. We left immediately. The second had deep crevices between great rocks. Crevices down which you could easily lose a small child or kill a nearly blind grown-up. The cottage was mustard-coloured. We did not linger there, either.

Once we were in the car, I was so dejected that Mother, against her own better judgement, said, "Well, I suppose you won't be satisfied till we take a look at that island."

We found Utterson eventually, drove up to a farm and followed Norman Longhurst to the property which, he told us, was the "most beautiful bit of land in Muskoka."

The sun was nearing the western horizon as we drove down the lane to the point. Everything was bathed in a golden light. And there was a special hush, a beauty we were not prepared for.

There was no cottage. But the ridge was crowned with soaring pines. From it the land sloped down, green and hummocky, to shelving granite rocks slanting down into blue water. Mr Longhurst assured us that right close to the shore the water was deep enough to dive into. Then we went on to the tip of the point, and there was the island.

Small. Dreaming. Private.

You could wade out to it. Yet it was a quite separate kingdom.

I'd call it Lilliput, I thought.

I knew how I would have loved it if I were a child. I loved it so much still. But it seemed to have been placed there especially for children.

"Nine thousand dollars," Mr Longhurst told us.

Before leaving home, we had agreed that the highest we could go was five. We did not have nine thousand dollars. And we would need a cottage. Without looking at each other, we shook our heads.

"Well, you think about it," he said. "I have somebody else coming to see it the day after tomorrow, though."

"Could we stay here and eat our picnic supper?" Mother asked.

"Sure," he said.

We sat side by side on the sun-warmed rock, looking out over the still lake. It was hushed, as though the two of us were alone in the world. I could not remember ever having loved any place so much. We ate in silence.

Then we started going over the selling points. Right

in front of where we sat, the water was deep enough
to dive into, perfect for swimming. At the tip of the
point, between it and the island, was a line of rocks
in an improvised bridge or dam. This had created a
small cove that was shallow and sandy. Ideal for little
children who could not swim. There was lots of space
for older children to play. There was the island.

"Imagine owning an island," I said softly.

We climbed the ridge again, both of us thinking
hard. Without Mother's backing, I could not find the
money. Young writers can't get loans. We got into the
car. Then we just sat for a long moment, looking back
at the place we both already loved.

Finally my sensible mother sighed.

"I guess this is it," she said.

My heart leapt but I did not dare believe.

"The money . . ." I murmured.

"We can borrow it," Mother said. "You can trade in
that insurance policy your dad got for you, too."

I might have known that Dad would be in on this.
He was always wanting to buy land, building dream
houses.

An hour later, driving south again, we told Mr
Longhurst to have the deed prepared.

That summer the whole family came. We put up
tents. I built, inside mine, a bookcase of bricks and
boards. We had a cabin built. It became the centre for
family holidays.

Seldom was I there with a single niece or nephew.
But never have I regretted making the decision to buy
the land.

A year later, Jamie and Hugh — one a banker, the
other a doctor — built a three-bedroom tongue-and-
groove cottage. It has housed many an uproarious

group of kids and has welcomed single people, too, needing a time of healing alone.

That first summer I wanted to christen my property. My favourite places in books all had names. Misselthwaite Manor. Toad Hall. Green Gables. Lantern Hill.

Many names were suggested and discarded. Then one day I remembered the words of a beloved spiritual.

> *There is a balm in Gilead*
> *Which makes the wounded whole.*
> *There is a balm in Gilead*
> *Which heals the sin sick soul.*

Gilead. That was it.

Gilead.

❧ 10 ❧

It's easy to invent a Life—
God does it — every Day—
Emily Dickinson

I was a guest author at the 1967 Cleveland Children's
Book Fair when a stranger told me casually that Miss
Jones would soon retire.

"I think she's going on working with a few of her
writers," someone else put in hastily, seeing how
shocked I was by the news.

In spite of being treated like a celebrity, I felt like
an imposter. But my association with Helen Jones, "my
editor," gave some substance to my belief in myself as
a genuine writer. If this news about her was true, who
would take her place? Could anyone?

That evening, while I sat on a couch listening to a
lady tell about her son's bar mitzvah, Ellen Rudin, an
editor with Harper & Row, sat down beside me. If I
talked things over with an editor . . .

The lady drew breath. Ellen was rising to go. I burst
out, "We met earlier. I'm Jean Little. I'm published by
Little, Brown."

"I know," Ellen said, settling back and smiling at me.

Although I had had five books published, I had
never struck up a conversation with an editor before.
Miss Jones had edited my work by mail from Boston.
To me, editors were remote beings with iron whims.
Actually chatting with one was unnerving.

Ellen's quiet warmth eased my tension. I made a feeble joke. She chuckled. My heart stopped thudding. Ellen did not think my concern was ridiculous or even unusual. She was sure that things would soon get straightened out. Ten minutes later I felt as though she and I had been friends always.

When I got home, it was almost time for the church bazaar. Every November the Chalmers United Church Women had a Christmas bazaar for which the members baked, preserved, smocked, knitted or created tree ornaments. Each woman donated her time and skill to raise money for the Mission and Service Fund of the United Church. Since my craft was writing, I had for several years put together a handmade book of poems or short stories.

I now selected an eight-page Christmas story called "The Gift," which I had written when I was in high school. I would have to expand it, but that would not be difficult.

Anna Solden, the nine-year-old heroine, was a German child who moved to Canada with her family in 1934. Only when the five Solden children had to have a medical examination before starting school did her parents learn that she had impaired vision. Glasses helped, but she still could not see well and had to attend a Sight Saving Class. She was a thorny, withdrawn little girl. My story told of how being part of this special class with its understanding teacher led to her gradual transformation into a happier child. As I worked on "The Gift," it grew from its original eight pages into forty-five.

I called the book *From Anna*. I loved the prickly child who, like me in grade two, wove a spectacular wastepaper basket as a Christmas gift for her parents. I liked the revised story so much that I sent Ellen Rudin a copy as a gift, and Helen Jones one asking her to consider it for possible publication.

Ellen loved Anna. Miss Jones wrote, too. *From Anna* was a charming story but not publishable as a book. Why didn't I try submitting it to a magazine and send her instead a book for my "usual audience"?

I glared at her letter. She had a perfect right to reject my story, but she must know it was too long for a magazine. Also I was irked with being told I had to stick to my usual audience. My readers were no homogeneous clump. If a very different book came to me "asking to be written," I wanted to be free to try. More than free. Encouraged.

What should I do? The years I had worked with Helen Jones had been deeply satisfying. I remembered how I had glowed when she had called *Home from Far* "beautifully disciplined." She had taken a chance on an unknown writer and taught her so much.

But she was retiring. Her reaction to *From Anna* plus her imminent retirement started me thinking about my future. Ellen Rudin and I had by this time exchanged two or three letters — not editor-author ones, but simply joyful notes between two friends. We talked the same language, laughed at the same human quirks, got elated about the same books.

I wrote to her blowing off steam about Miss Jones' response to *From Anna*. I had, in fact, just finished writing two manuscripts for my "usual audience" — a novel and its brilliant sequel about the same characters, Emily and Kate. I had planned to send both books off to Little, Brown as soon as they were done. Yet I delayed, waiting for word from Ellen.

Ellen's answer came. If Miss Jones was not interested

in *From Anna*, Harper & Row might be. "It would require some work," she said, "but you know that yourself." She would write details soon.

Ellen about the time I met her.

I waited, knowing in my heart of hearts that I was about to change publishers. By letting Miss Jones see *From Anna*, I had fulfilled the conditions set forth in my contract. If Harper & Row really wanted Anna's story, I'd send them Emily's and Kate's, too.

Ellen's official letter showed tension to match mine.

Well, here goes everything.

About From Anna, *we do think you can make it into an awfully good book if you are willing to try. . . .*

Several of us have now read the manuscript, and we

all find in Anna herself the germ of a truly memorable character. . . . but as of now, you have barely tapped her; and I think you will need to bring her forth, so that she can emerge whole and kicking in her own right.

. . . Just now From Anna *is not really a book in which things take time to happen; rather, it is a short narrative in which things are told about from a distance. It needs lots more dialogue. (Do you realize that Anna does not say a word until page 10! and yet we have been told zillions of things about her by then.) And it needs whole, realized scenes instead of sentences. For example, look at the possibilities for development in the following:*

> *"They knew that she was no good at games and that she scowled all the time, even on her birthday." (p. 1)*

> *"They were even fond of her . . ." (p. 1)*

> *"The new glasses came." (p. 4)*

She quoted other phrases. I saw exactly what she was getting at. I skimmed on down the page.

Along with this expansion, you might also consider a shift in focus, more toward Anna. We (you too) are agreed that it is Anna's own story, and perhaps it should be less general and more directly about Anna. Her point of view. How does Anna feel, for instance, when friends of the family "talk about the Solden children" and always compare her unfavorably with her brothers and sisters? She must hate it. What goes on in Anna's mind knowing, day after day, that she is "different" and not as good? She retreats, yes, we see that; but by what process and in what way? Is she really beaten down or does she have dreams of triumph? . . . And what is it in Anna that makes Papa believe that, "One of these

days, she'll show us all." The glasses change Anna.
So does school. But why, how? You know, and I think
even I know; but your reader won't know unless you
show him.

She wanted more about Miss Williams, Anna's
caring teacher.

. . . It is hard to believe Miss Williams is wonderful
without seeing it ourselves, without being able ourselves
to watch Anna open to Miss Williams' touch. "Miss
Williams did things exactly the way Anna thought
things should be done." Show us please, please; don't
just tell us. . . .

It went on for three pages. I reached the end and
sat staring at what she had said with surprise, irritation
and a singing delight. This New York editor I had barely
met knew Anna as well as I did. Not only knew her
but loved her. And, though I longed to argue, I longed
even more to start writing. Miss Jones' intelligent,
detached letters had delighted me but had never given
me the feeling that we were joined in an equal partner-
ship. I'd be a better writer working with Ellen. Bits of
this letter would keep sounding in my mind for years
to come. Already I saw how to begin.

Writing to Miss Jones took me the rest of the day.
The wastebasket overflowed with false starts before I
got it done. Once I had posted the letter, I sent the two
manuscripts — three hundred pages — to Ellen at
Harper & Row.

I was at Gilead, busy being an aunt, when her letter
reached me. Her salutation was a magnificent opening
shot in a long, disarming epistle that resulted in my
putting Anna aside and turning my two books into one

called *Look Through My Window*. This historic letter
began:

Dear Miss Galsworthy,

It ought to have been painful. It wasn't. I had never
had such fun writing. *Look Through My Window* is the
story of two girls from different backgrounds, who
become close friends. As Ellen and I sent letters back
and forth during its revision, Kate and Emily's deepen-
ing friendship became symbolic of hers and mine.

I had casually invented Kate Bloomfield before Ellen
and I met. Her father was Jewish, her mother a lapsed
Anglican. Kate was supposed to be a secondary character. Yet from the moment she walked into my head,
she refused to play a bit part. Ellen, being Jewish herself, took a special interest in all the Bloomfields.

Emily and Kate were poets. Their friend Lindsay
wrote, too, but badly. I had a wonderful time thinking
up poems for each. Lindsay's one effort was deplor-
able. Emily's resembled poems I had written at her age.
Kate's were mostly in free verse. I especially enjoyed
doing hers because they were poems I might have
written when I was twelve or thirteen, if I had not been
taught in school that poetry ought to rhyme, scan and
be about daffodils and skylarks. At fourteen, I longed
to write serious sonnets. (At fifteen, I accomplished
it. My first one began: "How the dark cup of sleep
eludes my lips.")

Kate's first poem started:

When I opened my eyes this morning,
The day belonged to me.
The sky was mine, and the sun,
And my feet got up dancing.

Hers were definitely more fun. Not that I couldn't write light-heartedly. In December 1969, I wrote Ellen that I would turn thirty-eight the following week. In her return letter, she reminded me that Elizabeth Taylor was also soon to celebrate her thirty-eighth birthday. Ellen recalled how Liz had been, in "National Velvet" and "Lassie Come Home," a child like the rest of us. What a shock when, overnight, she had grown up and acquired a bust.

I wrote back.

On Learning That Elizabeth Taylor and I Are Practically the Same Age

A couple of hundred years ago,
— Alas, I remember when! —
Elizabeth Taylor loved Lassie
And had yet to discover men.

Elizabeth lived with her mother,
Just as I lived with mine;
So valiantly she was Velvet
Crossing the finish line.

Elizabeth had a chipmunk
Called Nibble (I think) and tame;
I had a cocker spaniel.
Oh, we were SO the same

The two of us strolled towards growing up
Through childhood, slow and sweet;
But Elizabeth turned the corner
Before I got to the street.

Elizabeth flew like a ping pong ball
From one man to another.
Elizabeth was a femme fatale
While I still lived with Mother.

Elizabeth reached the Wide Screen
And not just in travelogues.
Liz was a cat on a hot tin roof
While I still played with dogs.

Elizabeth, dear Elizabeth,
What endless flings you've flung
I'm afraid you made a great mistake
Starting to age so young.

Remember her having pneumonia.
Remember her Oscars — two.
Remember her style on the River Nile
And the subsequent hullabaloo.

Think of her husbands! Look at her kids!
Her yachts! Her diamonds nifty!
With all she has to look back upon,
She MUST be fully fifty.

Oh, Elizabeth's lived with a capital ''L'';
She's been so long alive
That I feel maybe half her age
— Which makes me twenty-five.

My goodness, only twenty-five . . .
Still it's high time I got busy.
I have a thing or two to do
If I'm to catch up to Lizzie.

Look Through My Window came out, and I began work on *From Anna*. It was much harder than I had expected. When I sent Ellen my second draft, though, I thought I had followed her instructions to the letter. I waited for the accolades.

No ecstatic letter came winging back from New York.

"That's strange," I muttered. "She's had it for two whole weeks!"

Then Kate helped Ellen out by writing more poetry. I was startled. Much as I liked Kate, I had decided not to write a book about her because I was not Jewish. Scribbling down a few of the girl's poems was different, though. Ellen would enjoy them. I certainly did. I sent off three, then five. Soon Kate had written two dozen.

Then, lying in bed, I suddenly grasped what Kate was up to. Her poems were lengthening. New characters were appearing. Sheila Rosenthal, for instance. Something about her worried Kate.

"They're characters," I whispered. "Sheila is the first Jewish girl to join Kate's class. And Kate dislikes her . . ."

I lay there, my eyes wide, my brain whirling. Kate Bloomfield was trying to get me to write a book. Could I? In her voice?

I began right after breakfast. Writing in the person of Kate was fascinating. I had so much to figure out. Did Kate know how it would end? Why was she telling the story and to whom? Had Charlotte Bronte fussed about this while writing *Jane Eyre*?

I typed like mad. On the third day I knew I'd finish it before night. It would be too short and rough, but I knew it lived.

"Jean," Mother called up the stairwell, "the mail's here."

I ran down. A letter from Ellen. I pulled out the single sheet and stared at the brief message. I could feel my eyes pop.

> *Dear Jean,*
>
> *I think Kate wants to write her own book. Think about it.*
>
> > *love,*
> > *Ellen*

I typed faster and, just before supper, completed the first draft. Sixty-seven pages. But almost everything that mattered was down on paper. I ached all over but I was blissful. I ate, excused myself and phoned Ellen.

She would not let me read her all sixty-seven pages over long distance. I sent the manuscript to her the minute the post office opened the next morning. Special delivery.

After forever, Ellen wrote to me about *Kate* and *From Anna*. They wanted all sorts of changes in Anna's story. I could not believe it. I would have been devastated if I had not already begun turning the rough draft of *Kate* into a full novel. Again I pushed Anna aside. She was not surprised. She had played fifth fiddle all her life.

When, finally, *Kate* was done and I turned back to Anna, I was appalled at Ellen's list of suggestions. She wanted me to begin the story much earlier. She wanted to know more about Anna's classmates, more about Papa's store, more about Rudi. She was crazy!

I wrote a third draft. Now she would surely love every word.

"Jean, I think we still need to back up," she wrote. "We need to see this family in Germany . . ."

"No! Please, no!" I groaned.

With the next draft I sent, I enclosed this plea for mercy.

The More Poem

MORE about the new house!
MORE about the store!
MORE about Papa!
MORE! MORE! MORE!

MORE about Gretchen!
And, please, just add

Another encounter
With that eldest lad.

MORE about Frieda!
It can't be true.
More about ANNA
You're wanting, too?

How about Mama
And poor, old Fritz?
Well, she's alcoholic
And he has fits.

And I now warn you,
We'll have War
If you dare ask for
One more MORE!

Back came a letter that was heaven to read.

> . . . *congratulations on the final revision of* From
> Anna. *I knew you could do it, and you have, not just*
> *well but beautifully . . .*

She went on to praise specific bits, and I read the
letter several times, beaming.

That night I was at a church meeting.

"How's the writing?" one of the women asked
politely.

"Oh, it's glorious," I said and, forgetting that my
listeners had the bazaar book, told of the various revi-
sions of *From Anna.*

"Well, I liked your story exactly the way it was," one
friend sniffed. "You shouldn't let that woman force you
to change things."

The whole group murmured their agreement.

"It isn't like that," I began. "Ellen doesn't force me.

A writer can get too close to her work and can't be objective. Like a mother."

They laughed. "But don't you mind?" Ethel asked.

"Sometimes." I recalled occasions when an editor had infuriated me. "But if *they* miss my point, the readers likely will, too."

"It must be lovely to have stories come bubbling out," Mabel said sweetly. "I don't know how you do it."

Bubbling out! *From Anna* had taken me years and years and years. It had cost me sleepless nights, given me migraines, turned my hair grey. I opened my mouth to tell her off.

Then I realized that I would not have missed writing Anna's story for anything. Mabel was absolutely right. It had been lovely.

ꙮ 11 ꙮ

The Habit of a Foreign Sky
We — difficult — acquire
Emily Dickinson

As my friend Anne Reuber and I drove down the gravel
road to town to pick up supplies for Silver Lake United
Church Camp, I sang softly a song I loved from the
Medical Mission Sisters album, "I Know the Secret."

> *Paul was a Hebrew by birth.*
> *He left his land to inherit the earth.*
> *He sowed God's Word, and when the seed gave yield*
> *In the hearts of a few, he bought the whole field . . .*

Anne wasn't singing. At the end of the verse, I asked
her what was wrong.

"Nothing's wrong," she said. "Awhile back, though,
you were talking about next year. Well, I might not be
here. I'm planning to go overseas somewhere."

"Overseas? Where? What to do?" I demanded.

"To teach English or music maybe. Whatever they
want. I haven't applied yet, but I'm planning to."

"You mean, go somewhere for five years?" I said,
amazed.

"No," Anne said. "I would go for a short term with
CUSO maybe. If they accept me, that is."

Perhaps I was inspired by the Apostle Paul's example
in the song I'd been singing. Perhaps I simply couldn't

bear to be outdone by Anne. Perhaps I wanted to give her a shock to equal the one she had just given me. Perhaps, now that I had turned forty, I wanted to prove I had not lost my sense of adventure. But I truly believed I was joking when I said the words that were to change our lives.

"Maybe I'll come along. After all, I can write anywhere. All I need is a place to plug in my typewriter. And it would be exciting to try living in a different culture."

The idle words created possibilities I had not considered until that moment. Although I had travelled widely, I had not lived out of North America since I was seven. Maybe I really could go somewhere else for a time.

Anne had still not applied to CUSO when she happened to pick up a copy of the *United Church Observer* in our bathroom and read that the church also needed people to serve abroad on a short-term basis. Off went her letter asking for information. The Division of Mission found her more than acceptable. They decided to send her to Zambia.

Since I came of missionary stock, my wish to accompany her was less surprising than it might have been. My maternal grandparents had gone out to Taiwan in 1892, long before there were daily plane flights or telephone lines that could speedily bridge the widest ocean. My parents had been working in Taiwan as medical missionaries when I was born, and Aunt Gretta had spent fifty-one of her seventy-three years there.

Anne's parents stood up to the plan heroically. If my mother had her doubts, she kept them to herself. And, little by little, my crazy idea became a definite plan. Whatever the Division of Mission or our assorted friends and relations thought about it, they all eventually agreed that it would be nice for Anne to have my company and interesting for me to have the experience. I committed myself to stay for the entire three and a half years, although inwardly I knew that I could always turn tail and come home if it didn't work.

When we thought we were bound for Zambia, I was relieved. I would be able to communicate with most Zambians in English. We bought sandals, read books, applied for passports. I was visiting Anne in Stratford that May, when she came home from school and gave me a funny look. "I got a phone call today," she said. "Zambia can't pay my salary. We're going to Japan."

"Japan," I echoed blankly. "But we didn't buy winter coats. And they'll speak Japanese."

"We'll go to language school for the first six months," Anne reassured me.

I was not comforted. Judging by my inability to master the rudiments of French or Latin, I was not gifted at languages. Yet it was too late to back out.

He bought the whole field for joy, an inner voice reminded me.

Shut up, I growled at it. Yet I made tapes of all my Medical Mission Sister albums. I was going to need those songs.

We landed in Tokyo after dark. As we drove through the crowded, noisy, brightly lit streets on the way to our apartment, I tried my best to feel a sense of adventure, but I was too bone-weary. I yearned for my own bed in my own room in my own country. I could not understand why the missionary who had come to meet us kept peering through the taxi windows and sounding muddled. Why didn't she simply tell the man our address?

Only later did I come to understand that this was the first of many things in Japan that operated totally differently from the like situation in Canada. Japanese houses are not necessarily numbered consecutively. It is not the street that is given a name but the block or district; even the Japanese people who have lived in the same town all their lives cannot locate a house simply by being given its street address. Our guide had been to our building before and she was now searching for landmarks.

"Futaba Mansion," she called out suddenly. "There it is."

Feeling dazed with fatigue and utterly alien, lugging our various unwieldy bags, we trailed after her into an apartment block that bore no resemblance to a mansion, as we knew the word.

Once we get into our own place, I told myself, everything will be better. And no matter what it's like, there'll be a bed.

I had never fully appreciated the luxury of a bed till then.

But the apartment we were ushered into was gloomy and unwelcoming. The three rooms opened out of one another like a row of train cars. The furniture was black and massive. The only light came from a fluorescent bar in the ceiling. It looked cold, and the bluish light it cast was inadequate. The noise outside the single window, at the end of the room furthest from the door, was deafening. And there were no beds!

I sank down on a straight chair and had what felt like three headaches simultaneously. Why on earth had I come?

While I moped and Anne stayed doggedly cheerful, the missionary showed us the Japanese beds, folded up in a large wall cupboard with a sliding door. She and Anne dragged them out and began to make them up with bedding we had brought with us. I eyed the skinny mattresses askance.

A knock sounded on our door. Two women, their hair wet from swimming, came in and smiled at us. The first lady introduced everybody. I could not seem to get clear who they were.

"You poor things," the one called Julie said. "You look dead."

Had she said she was a nun?

The short one, Janet, surveyed our bleak domicile.

"What you need is a toaster," she said, "and a fan. And better futon. I'll take you shopping tomorrow."

Anne was polite. I tried to be. They left. With hardly a word, Anne and I toppled onto our respective futon. Mine was thin and lumpy. It felt heavenly. I fell headlong into an exhausted sleep.

The telephone woke us. Anne scrambled over to it and answered. It was Jean Kellerman, a longtime friend of her parents, bidding us welcome and inviting us to come to Hokkaido for Christmas. It was very hot in the apartment that September morning. Christmas seemed years away. But her kindness made everything easier. We had a friend in exile.

That afternoon, we watched with awe as Janet bought us our fan, our toaster and new foam rubber mattresses and downy quilts. It was a whirlwind trip. When we returned home at four o'clock, Anne and I ran out of steam.

"All I want is to sleep," I moaned. "It feels like midnight."

"I'm going to try our Japanese bath first," Anne said.

She turned it on. We ignored the sun shining in through our window and put on our pyjamas. After all, the day before had lasted nearly forty hours. I took out my plastic eye. The air pollution was going to make it uncomfortable, I could tell.

Suddenly I wondered if my electric typewriter would work here.

"Try it," said Anne.

I typed the thing about the quick brown fox. It worked fine.

Bang, bang, bang. Somebody was hammering on our door.

We stared at each other in alarm. Who . . .?

"You go," I said.

"We'll both go," Anne told me.

Neither of us remembered that I had only one eye in my head. We opened the door a crack and tried to hide our pyjamas behind it.

A woman in a dark-blue house dress yelled at us. Not one word could we understand. We stared at her helplessly.

"We made too much noise with the typewriter," I guessed.

The lady threw up her hands and dashed away up the hall. We closed the door and started discussing how I could type silently.

Bang, bang, bang, BANG!

I remembered my eye this time and jammed it in before we again opened the door. A man in dark pants and an undershirt had taken the lady's place. He greeted us politely, but he looked tense.

"Let's show him the typewriter," I suggested.

We led him across our two beds which took up most

of the floor space. We switched on the typewriter. He nodded courteously.

"Ah, so," he said. "Typewriter. Very nice."

Then he bolted into our bathroom and turned off the water. At last, through pantomime, he made us understand. Our ofuro was cracked. We were flooding the apartment beneath ours.

We apologized as profusely as possible. He gallantly kept from staring at our night attire. We closed the door once more and collapsed in gales of nervous laughter. What a start to our stay in Japan! How embarrassing! What must the poor man be thinking?

In the next few months, as we continued to make error after error, we came to know what he thought. Crazy foreigners!

We did not come close to mastering Japanese in our months at the Naganuma Language School, but we did learn how it felt to struggle with phrases and sentences that made no sense. We emerged with a smattering of Japanese and a real empathy for our students.

I was sitting there one morning, bored by the endless reiteration of sentence patterns, when the teacher asked me in Japanese, "How many eyes have you?"

I grinned at her and, reaching into my purse for my spare plastic one, answered, "Three."

When I placed it on the desk in front of her, she let out a memorable shriek. It was a lively moment in a deadly lesson.

When I had first gotten my plastic eye nine years before, I would not have believed it would ever turn into an asset, let alone be a subject for jokes.

Soon I knew my way to the supermarket, to Janet's and Julie's, to the church, even to the Naganuma School. But it was time I stayed home and did some writing.

I tried. The apartment was so quiet. I talked Anne into buying a dog.

We found her in a pet shop. She was a tiny Pomeranian with brains enough to lick Anne's cheek lovingly the moment they met.

"She kissed me," Anne said in such a besotted voice that I knew no more persuasion was needed. We named her Missy.

Then Anne was sent to teach English as a Second Language in a Hokuriku Gakuin, a Christian school in Kanazawa. We moved in April. Although I missed our friends in Tokyo, I liked our Kanazawa apartment with its large bright windows. I convinced Anne that, since I spent my days at home, I should be allowed to keep my futon out all day instead of tucking it away in the bedding cupboard.

"I sit and think on it," I insisted.

Missy kept giving me away by going back to bed just as Anne was leaving for school.

The morning after we moved in, I decided to take Missy for a walk around the block. We set out promptly at nine. We walked to the corner, turned left and left again and headed back. But we did not arrive. The apartment seemed to have vanished off the face of the earth. The street did not look the same, either. I kept going, expecting to get my bearings at any moment. Missy trotted along happily, enjoying the smells of this new place. The sun shone. The sky was vivid blue. It was a perfect April day. But at last I stopped walking and checked my watch. It was past ten. We had spent over an hour trying to get back to our starting point.

"We're lost, Missy," I said.

Her feathery tail vibrated joyously. She loved being

lost. I thought hard. No glimmer of an idea came. I started walking again.

I searched for landmarks. Every gateway we passed seemed to lead into a courtyard containing a stone lantern. We passed two or three Japanese. I did not ask for help. Even if they understood me, which was unlikely, I would not understand their instructions.

Surely, eventually, I would meet another foreigner.

I met two. They were Mormon missionaries who had been in Kanazawa only a week. They spoke not a word of Japanese. They had no idea where Nagamachi Ni-Chome was. I accepted their sympathy and kept going.

Finally I spotted the hotel where we had eaten the day before. Home was ten minutes away, and I knew how to get there. As I entered our building, I checked the time. Our walk around the block had taken my dog and me over three hours.

Grace Robertson, a long-time resident of the city, arrived five minutes later for lunch. I explained why lunch was not ready, and she told me why Kanazawa has only two or three through streets. It was planned that way in medieval times so that the ruler, in the temple at the highest point in the city, would see his enemies trying to find their way through the maze of dead-end streets and still have lots of time to prepare for battle.

I began working on my novel *Stand in the Wind*. It was not about Japan. With the possible exception of my two novels about Anna, it is the most Canadian of any of my books.

"I thought you'd write a story set in Japan," everyone said.

But I could not write a book about children whose

language I could not speak. I could not even eavesdrop as I rode the bus or passed a playground or went flower-viewing. Children all around me laughed, sang, teased and squabbled, but I was shut outside.

Only once did I overhear and take in an entire conversation. In the train seat behind me, a mother was travelling with a very small boy. He looked out the window and saw a river.

"Kaba," he said proudly.

Although his mother was leafing through a magazine, she glanced up, saw what he saw and set him straight.

"Kawa," she told him. He did not believe her.

"Kaba," he corrected in his turn, his high voice very certain.

I, looking back, saw her smile. She shook her head at him.

"Kawa," she said firmly.

He stared up at her and slowly repeated, "Kawa?"

This time she nodded vigorously. "Hai, kawa," she said.

The child repeated, "Kawa," submissively. Then he turned his back on her and leaned his forehead against my seat. Only I heard his small, obstinate voice softly chant, "Kaba, kaba, kaba, kaba," under his breath.

I laughed aloud. And, all at once, I wanted to be with my nieces and nephews who, while I was away, were growing up fast. I longed to be closer to Ellen Rudin and to my readers. Much as I enjoyed my years in Kanazawa, much as I came to value our Japanese friends, I returned to Canada a year before Anne. I had other good reasons but, really, it was simply that I needed to be at home.

I, like Emily Dickinson, had had trouble acquiring the habit of a foreign sky.

I unpacked, did a last edit on *Stand in the Wind* and settled back to wait for the central character in my next book to walk into my head and say, "Write about me."

The one person I did not expect to see was Anna Solden.

⚔ 12 ⚔

The Bravest — grope a little—
And sometimes hit a Tree
Directly in the Forehead—
Emily Dickinson

Rudi Solden was thirteen in 1934. In 1939 he must have been eighteen, old enough to enlist. What had he done? Once this question occurred to me, I could not stop wondering.

At last I sat down at the typewriter. I'd drop in on the Solden family. A few pages should settle it. I began to write.

> *Anna wakened to hear someone walking from the bathroom back along the hall.*
> *"Is that you, Papa?" she asked.*

I was in the Soldens' house on the morning of Sunday, September 5, 1939, the day Britain declared war on Germany. Before I finished that one page, I knew I had to stay.

"I've started another book about Anna," I told Mother, my amusement and amazement both clear in my voice.

"Good," she said. "So many children have asked for a sequel."

"But she's fourteen now."

"They won't mind that," said my mother.

While I was at work on the manuscript, Ellen Rudin left Harper & Row and, later, took an editorial job with E. P. Dutton. I wanted to go on working with her, so my new book went to Dutton, too.

From Anna had been hard to write, but it had not required a great deal of research. A nine-year-old's world consists largely of school and home. But now Anna had started high school, and her new country had gone to war with her homeland. I spent long hours in the library checking on what the weather was like that historic Sunday, what movies were playing in Toronto, what things cost, where Hitler was born and what exactly would be done with Rudi once he became a naval recruit. Mother got motion sick reading microfilm. Even so, it was an easier book to write than *From Anna* because it had not begun as a short story and because I had been seven in 1939 and remembered clearly the small details that bring another time to life: waxed paper bread wrappers, the clop-clop of the milkman's horse, flickering black-and-white newsreels on Saturday afternoons, Churchill's indomitable voice coming from our radio.

The book ended with Anna helping Rudi to adjust to blindness. I used my own short-lived but frightening period of despair after the loss of my left eye. Rosemary's book had pulled me clear. Anna got her brother a Talking Book by Charles Dickens. Since Anna, not Rudi, was the central character in *Listen for the Singing,* I telescoped Rudi's adjustment into a couple of chapters. I knew that his troubles were not over at the end of the book, but I did not realize how facile those chapters might sound to someone newly faced with such a loss.

Although *Listen for the Singing* was my tenth published book, I as yet knew few Canadian children's writers. The writer I felt closest to was still Rosemary Sutcliff who lived half a world away. At this time, however, I helped found CANSCAIP, an organization unique in Canadian literary history. A group of us gathered in Port Colborne, Ontario, to speak to schoolchildren and ended up beginning the Canadian Society for Children's Authors, Illustrators and Performers.

I so longed to make friends with other Canadian writers that I should have been cheering for this new group. Wasn't this exactly what I had been hungering for ever since the publication of *Mine for Keeps*? Maybe — but that day I felt little kinship with the others. Only three of them had written novels. I said I doubted such a group would work. They wisely ignored me.

I had to leave early. Feeling slightly ashamed of my lack of enthusiasm, I paused at the door and said, "I still think you're crazy, but good luck. If I can help, I will."

I was the crazy one. CANSCAIP has become a national organization with hundreds of members. Living in Guelph and unable to drive in to meetings, it was several years before I fully appreciated what a good thing we had done that afternoon in Port Colborne.

Early in 1976, I noticed my remaining eye misting over for short periods of time. It didn't hurt. And it didn't last. I visited Dr Young, the ophthalmologist who had taken over my case. He checked the pressure, looked serious but said little. I did not press him. I did not want to be told anything alarming. My left eye had started misting over once in awhile when I was eleven, but had not developed blisters till I was thirty. My right eye was stronger, better, not as damaged.

Don't worry, I told myself.

I kept fear battened under for months. Then the fog got thicker and stayed longer. Within weeks the first small blister appeared. Mother and I went back to Dr Young. He sent me to consult a specialist in Toronto. Dr Moran peered into my eye for a long time. We waited. We both guessed what was coming, but it was still a shock.

"Glaucoma," he said matter-of-factly.

I was panic-stricken. The last time, once I started having blisters and the vision grew misty, it had ended a year and a half later in my having to have the eye removed. Losing my left eye had been bad, but I had still been able to see. This time I would have no spare eye left.

The doctor gave me drops to use. We went home stunned, disbelieving. I felt as though the world, reassuringly solid beneath my feet, had all at once tipped over and sent me spinning into space.

Yet we had supper. We did the dishes.

Maybe by this time next year I'll be blind, a cold flat voice kept repeating inside my head as I dried the cutlery.

Stop it, I told myself. Stop it right this minute. You are being melodramatic. You're building it up.

It was as useful as telling my tongue to stop poking at a bitten place on the inside of my cheek.

When I got a blister on my cornea that evening and covered my eye with a patch, I was in total darkness.

It will soon be like this all the time, the same cold voice insisted.

I went to bed at the usual hour. But it was getting

light outside the window before I slept.

The next couple of days were strangely unreal. I could still read for an hour at a stretch. Much of the time my vision was as normal as it had ever been. Yet I stared hard at trees and houses, cars and passing clouds until, gradually, mist would creep between me and the familiar world. I would hold my hand up and see a grey blur edging each finger. The lights had haloes. Automatically I would try to blink the fuzziness away. Stubbornly it went on clinging to things, outlining windows with a ghostly white, robbing the world of its clean edges, muting its strong, clear colours.

Wait. It will soon go, I reminded myself.

Often it did, sometimes after only a couple of hours.

But that return to what was familiar and usual did not dispel the horrors. Though I kept watching lights and windows for the reappearance of the mist, I never could get accustomed to it. How could I adjust to and accept something that came and went that way? And what if, some day, it just stayed?

More and more often, blebs formed. Pain would force me to put on that detestable plastic patch which kept my eye closed and quiet. It hurt less but it also blinded me.

I can't bear it, I would yell inside my head.

Then I would jeer at myself. After all, what choice had I? Think about really blind people, I snapped. They are in the dark all day and they manage. You don't catch them whining this way.

But they aren't writers, I argued. How will I write?

I had not yet discovered a sure way of silencing that question. Knowing that there were able blind writers — Ved Mehta, Beverly Butler, Robert Russell — did not help. If anything, thinking of them made things worse. I was convinced that their methods would not work for me. I needed to see the words in sentences and paragraphs, on pages of typing paper.

Two days after I had heard the diagnosis, the phone rang.

"Is this Jean Little?" said a voice.

"Yes," I said.

"I'm phoning to tell you that *Listen for the Singing* has won the Canada Council Children's Literature Prize."

I sat down abruptly on the chair next to the telephone table.

"It did?" My own voice sounded faint, disembodied, like someone else's. "I . . . I've never heard of it. What is it?"

One seldom gets to be the bearer of such joyful tidings. The unknown voice practically purred.

"It's five thousand dollars," she said. "Congratulations!"

I gasped. Then I laughed.

"Are you kidding?" I said, suddenly suspicious.

"No, of course not."

I pulled myself together. I did not explain that not only was I unaware of the award, I had no idea what the Canada Council was. The prize was to be given at a conference in Hamilton in about a month. Mother and I had planned to go to Vancouver and visit Pat and her family then. Well, Mother would just have to go without me.

For that month I almost succeeded in pushing the thought of losing my vision to the back of my mind. Almost. I did have another doctor's appointment, however, in the weeks between.

Before keeping it, I got a long dress. I invited friends to come with me, as the Canada Council suggested. It was going to be wonderful.

Then Dr Young put me on a new drug called Diamox. It had helped others, but in my case it had several disastrous side effects.

First, it shrank my tiny pupil so successfully that I could not see anything but a thick, dirty-yellow haze. It was the ugliest colour I have ever seen. Greyish-mustard. Second, it affected my balance. I walked drunkenly, staggering, having to steady myself on the furniture. Third, it sent me plummeting into a black pit of depression out of which I could not clamber, however hard I tried.

Since the drug was prescribed only the day before I went to receive the prize, we had not fully realized how catastrophic its effect was. Aunt Gretta and some friends and I found ourselves at a conference that seemed to be made up of math teachers. I was groggy, admittedly, but I did not understand one word the guest speaker said. I almost fell asleep at the table. I kept jerking my head up and forcing my leaden eyelids open. It did not help that he was showing slides.

Judy Sarick, the owner of the Children's Bookstore in Toronto, made a short, gracious speech and waited to hand me the cheque.

I got up, tripped over the hem of my dress, recovered myself, reeled up the three steps to the platform and accepted the envelope. Winning such an award just as I lost my vision had a bittersweet edge. Why didn't we Canadians celebrate our own kids' books? Why were my novels given fine reviews in *The Horn Book*, yet often ignored at home?

When I sat down, I thought muzzily about the

words I had just spoken. Had I really said, "I'm glad Canada has finally discovered me"? I couldn't have. But I was very much afraid I had.

Change was in the air, however. Good books written by Canadians and with Canadian settings were beginning to find their way into the hands of Canadian kids, despite the tardiness of such prestigious libraries as Boys and Girls House to make room on the shelves for them, and despite Sheila Egoff's pessimism in her book on Canadian children's literature, *The Republic of Childhood*. No longer were our children growing up believing that true heroes and heroines had to be British or, at least, American.

That evening in Hamilton should have heralded this dayspring. But for me it marked the onset of one of those nights Emily Dickinson referred to as "larger darknesses" — those "evenings of the brain" where no inner stars shine.

Sometimes such a night seems very dark before the first stars finally appear.

⚹ 13 ⚹

I lost a World — the other day!
Has Anybody found?
You'll know it by the Row of Stars
Around it's forehead bound.

A Rich man — might not notice it—
Yet — to my frugal Eye,
Of more Esteem than Ducats—
Oh find it — Sir — for me!
Emily Dickinson

Once I stopped taking Diamox, I could "see" my blurry world again. It went on fading out and reappearing but, in contrast to the mustard nothingness, it was beautiful to me. I was also relieved to recover my physical equilibrium and clarity of speech.

The frightening depression that the drug seemed to have precipitated did not go away, however. Trying to ignore it, I flew to Vancouver to join Mother.

My sister's family was in trouble. As tensions mounted and tempers flared, Mother and I tried to become invisible.

"Look at these," Pat said grimly, thrusting Mark's and Sarah's report cards into my hands.

I peered at the marks. No wonder she was upset! Both kids were on the point of failing their year. I, the ex-teacher, had not much comfort to offer.

"If I were going to be *here*," I said, marshalling a

dozen good reasons for not staying, "I'd offer to tutor them but . . ."

"How about taking them home with you?" said my sister. "I'd like them away from here. If you had them to yourself at Gilead . . ."

My mouth must have dropped open. I know I came close to yelling, "How can you ask this of me? Don't you understand that I'm going blind? I can't cope with my problems, let alone yours."

I bit back the words. Mother was looking at me, waiting for me to agree. I loved my sister and her children. Teaching them might give me a sense of purpose, even revive my sense of humour.

Mother, me and Pat.

Sarah and Mark approved this plan. It was only the end of May. By coming east, they would get out of an entire month in regular school. I foresaw trouble and drew up a contract that committed all of us to three hours of solid work every morning, Monday through Friday. Mother was roped in. We all four signed it. They scribbled their signatures joyfully. Mother and I exchanged rueful glances. This was going to be a summer to remember.

The moment we were back in Guelph, Mother solved the problem of what to do with my award money.

"What we really need," she told me briskly, "is a new car."

She would drive it for me, but it would be mine. The idea of my purchasing my first automobile just as I lost my sight had its darkly comic side. Nobody but my practical mother would have come up with such a notion at such a time. We chose a deep-red Dodge.

"I'll call her Scarlett," I said, "because my money is gone with the wind."

"Scarlett isn't enough of a name," Sarah told me. "Call her Scarlett Charlotte, Aunt Jean."

So Scarlett Charlotte she became.

The kids kept their word until the end of June. After they knew their friends in Vancouver were free from lessons, though, the four of us engaged daily in an uncivil war. I clung to the knowledge that autumn always comes eventually. Then, late in August, Pat called to break the news that she was leaving her husband and coming home to live in Guelph for awhile.

She and the kids found a place a short block away from our house. They stayed for a year. It was good to have them so near, yet it was not an easy stretch of time for any of us. We all had major adjustments to make, and it was hard to be patient with each other. Pat worried about her two older children, still in

Vancouver, and struggled to fit into a new nursing job. Sarah and Mark missed their father, their home and their friends and resented being ordered around by their aunt and their grandmother. I stayed locked in the dark prison of depression. Mother bore with us all.

"Pick up your feet, Jean," she said.

"I can't. They're too heavy."

"Nonsense," she snapped. "You're forty-six and you are dragging around as though you were Gretta's age."

My eyes filled with the tears that, those days, always seemed ready to spill over. My feet felt made of iron. To lift them and walk normally took immense effort. I was always tired, longing to sit or lie down. And it wasn't all in my head. It was real.

Mother looked at my tragic expression and sighed.

"I know it's hard," she said quietly, "but I think the answer is to keep busy. Feeling sorry for yourself won't help, you know."

Work. That was her remedy for everything. Why couldn't she understand that I tried and tried to work. Nothing I wrote was the least bit inspired. Nothing was worth keeping. Now that I had been given that Canada Council prize, I would probably never write a book again. Mother thought you could just go on churning out words, but she was wrong. Let her try it just once and she'd see.

"If I didn't have such a headache . . ." I mumbled and escaped to my room. I curled up on the bed, my back to the door, and pushed the Play button on my Talking Book machine. My tears dried as I retreated even further from all I could not yet face. *The Grand Sophy* by Georgette Heyer came romping to my rescue. How I wished more of her books were on tape. Sighted readers chose from a long list of titles. Only six of these were in the Talking Book Library of the Canadian National Institute for the Blind.

"I can't write if I'm expected to babysit Pat's kids while she's at work," I fumed at my mother later. "You take her job seriously but not mine. Nurses matter; writers don't."

"What do you want me to do?" My mother said wearily.

"Nothing," I raged and stamped up the street to my sister's.

What *did* I want her to do? I wanted her to take away my fear, to give me back those joyous days I had spent writing busily about Rudi's blindness and not fearing my own. I wanted her to make everything all right the way mothers were supposed to.

At last, driven crazy by my own inertia, I started trying to turn another short story into a novel. The first version of *Mama's Going to Buy You a Mockingbird* had been written before I went to Japan. It was about Jeremy Talbot, whose father had died of cancer. Adrian Talbot had loved Christmas, keeping up all the traditional customs and inventing new ones to delight his family. As the story opened, Jeremy wakened early on the holiday morning and, for the first time in his life, dreaded the day ahead. Then his memories led him to a new joy, more difficult yet deeper than any he had known before. I liked the Talbots so much that I wanted to give them a whole book to themselves. I had started on it and been interrupted. Now that I had to struggle both with failing vision and growing sorrow and rage, my story had lost its momentum.

Or I had lost mine.

Really I needed those weeks with Mark and Sarah to give me the heart of that book. Watching the two of them struggling to bear their loss of much that spelled home and, at the same time, experiencing my own loss of vision, which placed me, also, in an unfamiliar world, taught me much I needed to know to write *Mama's Going to Buy You a Mockingbird*. Their bickering, their love for Monopoly and for Gilead, their resentment of bossy adults all found their way into the manuscript.

But at the same time I knew only that whenever I could force myself to go to my typewriter, nothing much happened. Sitting and writing two pages of nothing much is far more exhausting than writing two good chapters. I told myself that I needed a rest. I lay on my bed and stared at the mist around the window. I cried a lot.

The haze thickened. I began to have trouble recognizing even my own family at close range. I confused Mother with Aunt Gretta. When the wrong one answered, it was often awkward.

I sent my water glass toppling, splashing its contents into the salad or over the bread. I started to fetch a towel. "Sit down. We'll do it," they said. "It could happen to anybody!"

I took a bite of potato. It was creamed whitefish. I had mashed butter into it. I ate it and wondered who had noticed.

I suddenly found the dishwater full of what felt like innumerable tea bags. I caught one of them and held it up to my face. It was a prune! The pot I had thought was "soaking" was really filled with prunes that Mother was cooking for supper.

One afternoon, when she and I were out in the garden, I asked her some question. When she failed to answer, I decided she had not heard me and went closer. She still would not reply. I was irritated until I got close enough to see her clearly. I had been yelling at the birdfeeder.

We laughed over the comical mistakes. We were grateful for them. Laughter was hard to come by just then.

"We grow accustomed to the dark," Emily Dickinson says. What she forgets to mention is how long it takes. I kept comparing the world around me to the much clearer world I had seen just months before. I tried to stop, but I could not. I often thought of Rudi Solden. I had had him emerge from his bitter isolation so readily. Why wasn't I being at least as courageous as Rudi? I had imagined all he had to do was listen to a Talking Book, learn Braille, go walking with Anna and be free. Ha!

My migraine headaches grew more frequent, more devastating. Under Mother's urging, I went back to see a Toronto doctor who had done his best to "cure" my headaches before. Perhaps he would have something new to try. Previously, no treatment had helped for more than a month or two. The doctor prescribed a drug that was used as a "mood elevator" but had also proved effective as a migraine preventative. I took the three small pills at bedtime.

When I wakened the next day, I felt as though I had been reborn. My feet were no longer leaden. My eyes were not brimming over with tears. All the enormous, overwhelming, soul-destroying problems confronting and defeating me had overnight become difficulties I could face, might even surmount some day. Was it the pills, or would it have happened anyway? Perhaps it was a little of both. But I did not care what had worked the miracle. I sat at the breakfast table and drank in the beauty of the sunlit morning and laughed with astonished joy.

"I feel new," I told Mother. "I feel like a different person."

"I can *see* the difference," Mother said, her voice husky. "It's written all over you."

All day I kept noticing the lightness of my feet. My migraines did not vanish, but the physical symptoms of depression never overwhelmed me that way again. Oh, there were bad times ahead still. But little by little, I found acceptance growing possible, troublesome new skills becoming second nature, my sense of humour returning, my real self resurrected. It took months and I had relapses, but the healing had started.

In my bedroom, bookshelves lined the wall from floor to ceiling. Hundreds of beloved volumes stood there, waiting for me to take them down. I tried to avoid noticing them, but I could not bear to have them removed. I needed their presence. Among them were books I had been buying for myself steadily since adolescence.

One evening, desperate to read, I found myself in front of the crowded shelves with my arms outstretched across the long rows of volumes, as though I were embracing them. I felt hunger, gratitude and a deep, sharp sadness. I suppose I was saying goodbye.

That winter and spring I even taught a children's literature course at the university, with much help from Mother and Pat. The students' respect for me bolstered up my sagging self-esteem much as five-year-old Alec had done years before by simply saying, "Good morning, Miss Little."

But there were testing times coming.

Several years before, I had taken my group of

Canadian Girls in Training to a concert given by the Medical Mission Sisters choir. We had sat in the front row and sang without having to look at the song sheets, because we knew all the songs by heart. The girls had known they were noticed, and they were pleased with themselves as they went up for autographs. I had spoken to Sister Miriam Therese Winter, the composer of both the words and the music, of what delight her songs had given me.

Immediately after I came home from Japan, I went to a workshop that she gave at Five Oaks, the United Church centre near Paris, Ontario. I had such a wonderful time that I returned to similar events led by her and Sister Mary Elizabeth Johnson ever since. Although we saw each other seldom, I had come to count on M. T. to start me writing poems, to share laughter-filled moments, to keep me singing, to renew my faith.

But now my life had altered. When I thought of attending the retreat she was scheduled to lead that June, I hesitated.

I wanted to see her, but wouldn't going to Five Oaks this time remind me painfully of all I had lost? But I longed to see M. T. I needed her strength and her songs.

Once there, I did try to dismiss disturbing memories, but they hung about me as persistently as the June mosquitoes. Then one night after darkness fell we all sat singing around a fire. Suddenly my eye began to sting. A blister! I fished out my plastic patch and gauze pads. Then I hesitated. I would be more comfortable with them in place, but I would also be totally blind.

The others began a new song.

Night is the promise of morning.
Night holds the key to the dawn.
Hope is a moment embedded with stars
That shine when courage is gone,
That shine when courage is gone.

My throat knotted and I stopped singing. Although no one was excluding me, I felt utterly shut out. I held onto the loneliness, nursing it, enraged by their joy, their blatant insensitivity. How dared they sit there singing away about "night"? What did they know about it?

"I'm tired," I said loudly, without waiting for the song to end. "I'm going to bed."

M. T. and a handful of others rose with me and wandered towards the main building. As we got beyond the circle of firelight and stood in the gentle summer darkness, she looked up and exclaimed in wonder, "What a glorious night! Just look at all those stars!"

As I tipped back my head, a couple of lines from one of Gerard Manley Hopkins' poems sounded in my memory.

Look at the stars! look, look up at the skies!
O look at all the fire-folk sitting in the air!

"Ohhhh," I heard the others gasp. "Ohhhh!"

The sky I saw was black, blank and lightless. I saw no stars at all.

I had noticed before that stars were harder and harder to see, but until that moment I had put it down to the sky being cloudy or the lights of the city being too strong. After all, I had never seen a skyful of stars on even my best nights. But I had always seen a scattered few, perhaps six, sometimes a dozen. I had seen more by looking through a monocular and had put together a mental image of the thronging brightness of the Milky Way. I loved stars so much that I had learned by heart poems about them and had written some of my own.

"I can't see a single star," I blurted. "Not one."

They were deeply sorry, but they went right on gazing up, seeing and seeing. They were my friends but, for that moment, I hated them.

The disappearance of the stars at once became a symbol to me of everything blindness was going to take from me in the years ahead. They were the first thing in my world to vanish totally. I still saw moving shadows which I knew were people. I still could make out individual words written in very black, clear print. I still could see doors and windows. Everything was blurry and misted over, but I retained a hazy image of my surroundings.

But no more stars.

Next it would be people or the houses across the street or trees. One by one, they were all going to fade out of sight. Already, when I stared at the back of my own hand, I could not see fingernails or the wrinkles that show where your knuckles are. Soon I would not see anything at all.

I fell back into despair. Weeks passed with me counting off the details I was losing.

Then, one afternoon, I lay on my bed just before supper, listening to Alexander Scourby reading Richard Adams' novel *Watership Down*. I had forgotten all about myself and my problems as I followed Hazel and his companions through their adventures. I was nearing the end and I hoped nobody would interrupt. I did not want to return yet. Then the beautiful voice read the last paragraph before the Epilogue.

> *A few minutes later there was not a rabbit to be seen on the down. The red sun sank below Ladle Hill and the autumn stars began to shine in the darkening east — Perseus and the Pleiades, Cassiopeia, faint Pisces and the great square of Pegasus. The wind freshened, and soon myriads of dry beech leaves were filling the ditches and hollows and blowing in gusts across the dark miles of open grass.*

How beautiful it is, I thought dreamily. How lovely.

Then my eyes popped open and I sat up. I had seen that starry sky clearly. Inside my head, the stars had pricked out one by one. This Talking Book about a bunch of rabbits had taken me across an ocean to Watership Down and revealed to me an autumn night in all its glory. Richard Adams and the CNIB Talking Book Library had given me back my lost stars.

I realized in that shining moment that I could see Northern Lights, coral reefs, prairie wildflowers, great forests, green hills, skyscrapers, even the wind in the willows whenever I liked. By merely pressing the Play button, I could leave behind the narrowing and dimming world my eye still glimpsed and lose myself instead in one that was as unlimited as the human imagination.

The darkness within me was not banished, but never since that afternoon has it seemed absolute or endless. I was ready, at last, to go forward.

⚔ 14 ⚔

When Night is almost done— . . .
It's time to smooth the Hair—

And get the Dimples ready—
And wonder we could care
For that old — faded Midnight—
That frightened — but an Hour—
Emily Dickinson

My diary entries for 1979-81 tell of enough ups and downs to make a roller coaster jealous, but bit by bit the ups became more frequent, the downs less terrifying. I was almost ready to begin learning how to be an expert blind lady.

The first sign that I was set to "get the dimples ready" came when a friend asked me to talk with a young man whose vision was poor but whose parents insisted he was not handicapped. He himself was muddled enough to refuse any help offered him by the CNIB and to avoid meeting disabled people. My friend was certain that talking things over with me would do him a world of good.

I doubted it. Unless the person in need of help is the one to set up the appointment, such encounters are not often profitable. His eyesight, I soon realized, was better than mine had ever been. Yet there he sat, hunched over, eaten up with self-pity. He was appalled by my fogs and blisters. His horrified gasps so annoyed me that I grew flippant. He was too shocked to respond in kind. Finally he blurted, "If I were you, I'd commit suicide."

At first I thought I had not heard him correctly. Then, understanding that he had betrayed his own secret nightmare, I tried to stay serious. I couldn't do it. I grinned instead.

"It's not that bad," I said. "As a matter of fact, I like my life a lot. I've never once considered parting with it."

It was true. Much as I still dreaded losing what was left of my sight, angry as I still was, my life remained infinitely precious to me. It was certainly not trash to be thrown away; it was treasure to be reclaimed. And it was time I got started.

I identified a list of problems I needed to solve before I could fully enjoy life again. I had to find a way to write. I had to learn how to go confidently outside my own four walls. I had to find games I could play, a craft that I could take pleasure in which had nothing to do with writing, a way to mark the appliances in our kitchen so they could be operated by touch, a way to label and store my rapidly increasing library of cassette tapes.

I was fairly good at laughing at the many mistakes I made daily. But why not find ways to prevent some from happening? I needed, for instance, a pepper shaker that could not be confused with the salt. I should get a bread knife that could measure off an even slice. And there must be untippable mugs.

Sick of looking pitiable and feeling helpless, I began to search for ways around those situations that made me feel blind. The first skill I had to recover was one I'd perfected long since but lately abandoned. Playing a part. I began pretending, once more, that I didn't mind not seeing; that I wasn't embarrassed by spilling things, running into people, writing one telephone message on top of another; that I liked life. I went back to bragging, showing off, making jokes, hoping for the best. It was a monumental relief to everyone I knew.

Next I had to find a way to write. For one thing, we needed the money. I had not had a new book out for several years. My royalties were still coming in but the cheques got steadily smaller. Writers, if they are to earn a living, must be prolific. I was having to accept every invitation to make a school visit or do a Canada Council "reading" at a library. I was a good speaker, but I wanted to give up talking ad nauseam about what it was like to be a writer and get back to being one.

Yet how could I free the time writing requires?

And if I did, how would I write in such a way that I could read over what I'd done?

I discarded Braille as a method. I had relearned it without much trouble, but I was painfully slow at it and I knew that it would be not months but years before my Braille skills could even come close to my typing speed. I had, after all, typed by touch since I was ten.

"I need a typewriter," I told Mother. "Perhaps I could get a machine with primer type big enough for me to see."

I found a standard electric typewriter with large type. I needed, I thought, a dictaphone, too. I needed the money to pay for the two machines and I also had to take time off from making school and library visits so that I could learn to write again. I had not touched *Mama's Going to Buy You a Mockingbird* for months. How would I manage?

Mary Rubio, one of the editors of the periodical

Canadian Children's Literature, had the answer. She persuaded me to apply to the Canada Council for a Senior Author's Grant. This grant helped me purchase the equipment and also gave me an allowance that paid some of the bills while I tried to write again. The Canada Council having enough faith in me to give this money helped to renew my faith in myself. I got Mother to read aloud what I had already done. I was secretly convinced that I would find the characters had lost all their vitality. But Jeremy and Sarah were still very much alive. I sighed with relief and went to work.

At first I tried actually writing onto the big type machine. But my sight grew misty and, however much I leaned over the keyboard, I could not decipher the words without rolling the sheet of paper out of the typewriter. Getting the paper back in so that I could go on right where I had left off was impossible.

I began dictating the first draft of each chapter into the dictaphone and then typing it. Once I had the manuscript pages in my hand, I would sit under a two-bar fluorescent light and flatten my nose against the paper to read over what I had done. For the words to be legible at all, I had to keep using brand-new heavily inked ribbons.

It was a frustrating process. When I would try retyping my work, since I could no longer see the words while the sheet was still in the machine, I was helpless when I made an error or when my finger accidentally hit the carriage return. I had to call for aid. If none was available, I'd gnash my teeth till someone came.

"Perhaps if I tape a bell onto the space bar and turn on a tape recorder and say each word aloud as I type it," I said to Mother, "I'll hear my mistakes and rewind the tape and listen to the noise of the keys, the whir of the carriage return and the ringing of the bell and just count back . . ."

"Isn't that a lot of trouble . . ." she began slowly.

I would not listen. "It'll work," I insisted. "It *has* to. I can't do it any other way."

It didn't work. It was complicated and silly and, even when I was careful, I whited out the wrong word or typed one line over top of another. I slammed down from the attic and threw myself on my bed and wept enraged tears.

Everyone stayed out of my way till the storm blew over.

Next I determined to dictate each chapter onto one tape and then, listening to that draft, rewrite onto another. I dictated without mentioning paragraphing or punctuation. I was convinced that it would be impossible to write a moving book saying, "Paragraph . . . quote . . . Can I come too . . . question mark . . . quote . . . said Sarah . . . period . . . paragraph . . ."

Nobody could write fiction that way. Nobody.

But, when I experimented to see if someone could transcribe my dictation, I myself kept putting in a period only to find that the sentence went on and I should have inserted a comma. If I, the writer, had trouble, how on earth would a typist manage?

I would have given up then if I had not needed to write so badly. I sat, glowering into space, when it came to me that, when I had been able to read, I had seen all those periods and exclamation points and quotes and they had never come between me and the story. My eye had interpreted them correctly without paying conscious attention to any of them. If my eye could do that, couldn't my ears perhaps do the same thing? Couldn't I hear as casually as I had once seen? And, even if it was hard at first, couldn't I train myself to do it in time?

That thought, half formed and hesitant, was what enabled me to finish *Mama's Going to Buy You a Mockingbird* at last. I went back to the first chapter and re-recorded it, putting in the punctuation marks and paragraphing. When I played the tape back, even the very first time, I found myself laughing at the jokes, wishing to change a phrase, excited and involved.

But did I really have to make a new tape every time I wanted to insert one sentence? I had discovered long since that it was impossible to amend the tape by recording over what was on it, talking faster the second time. You either went on several seconds too long, or you stopped short so that words repeated themselves.

I completed a whole draft making new tapes each time I wished to change anything. Then I learned how to use a jack. I no longer had to dictate the entire story six or eight times. I could let it record from the one tape to the other, jerking out the patch cord at the point where there was need to add or erase something.

It grew easier, but it was never easy, even when things went well. I embarked on the fourth, or was it the fifth, draft and tried not to think of how eagerly I had once hurried back to work. Now, every time, I had to force myself to return to the dictaphone.

"How can I remember exactly where anything is?" I demanded of anyone who would listen. "How can I keep from repeating myself without a text to leaf through?"

When people offered me solutions, I wanted to annihilate them. I didn't need their stupid ideas; I needed their sympathy. "I don't see how you keep at it," was the only acceptable response.

I had to keep at it if I wanted to go on being Jean Little. I slowly, painstakingly worked my way through to the end of a draft good enough to show to an editor.

I sent a copy to Ellen Rudin and another to Shelley Tanaka, an editor at Clarke Irwin. Then I waited for them to tell me whether I was still a writer.

Throughout these months, I went to more Medical Mission Sister weekends at Five Oaks. Each time I felt wonderfully at home there, even after I discovered that the stars had vanished. But I was having more and more trouble seeing.

When M. T. was slated to come later that summer, I hesitated about signing up. No friend was free to go with me. What if I got deserted while I was there? What if I got irretrievably lost? Maybe I should stay home.

I wrote to M. T. of my worries. She urged me to come. She was sure I would not be mislaid. Outwardly stalwart and cheerful, inwardly shaking like a jelly, I had someone drop me off at Five Oaks.

I did brush my teeth with shampoo, but that was the worst thing that happened to me. Time and time again, as I groped my way towards a chattering group, M. T. herself would call out a welcome. Time and time again, just as I began to feel lost, loving hands rescued me.

As M. T. told us about working with starving, war-weary refugees, I found myself touched in another sense. I began to grieve for the world's homeless and hungry instead of concentrating solely on my own woes.

Before I left Five Oaks, I wrote a poem called "In Touch" that expressed my new appreciation of caring hands and voices. I began by memorizing the lines as I composed them and, finally, wrote them down on foolscap with a thick black marker.

> *Creator God who simply spoke*
> *And mountains heaved and morning broke,*
> *Creator God, who with a word*
> *Fashioned ocean, cloud and bird,*
> *God who could have, from afar,*
> *Made people for this minor star*
> *Using just the power of speech,*
> *Remaining distant, out of reach,*
> *God I love and praise who came*
> *Yourself to hold and mould our frame,*
> *Forming us from common soil*
> *With joy and playfulness and toil,*
> *Saving this shaping till the end*
> *Thinking perhaps to find a friend*
> *For converse and for company,*
> *Finding instead your family,*
> *Teach us who draw back so much*
> *That love comes close enough to touch.*

I had written very little poetry in the two years leading up to that weekend. The few lines I had gotten down had been full of my pain, fear, aloneness and anger. My spirit, as well as my body, had lost its vision.

What a blessing it was to find myself able to end my poem with this affirmation of faith.

> *When, failing, in despair, we ask*
> *To pass to other hands the task*
> *Of healing, so beyond our power,*
> *Remind us in that anguished hour*
> *That you who fashioned us from dust*
> *Are with us still, have earned our trust,*
> *And share with our humanity*
> *Not only lonely agony,*

Not only morning, star and bird
But, if we take you at your Word,
Love that's not just dutiful
But jubilant and beautiful,
Love that sings while suffering
Because love cannot help but sing.
When the world's pain becomes so great
We rage or weep or turn to hate,
Redeem us even as you planned.
Give us the grace to understand
You have us still within your hand.

Ellen and Shelley both wrote about the manuscript. Ellen's letter was unofficial, since she was no longer publishing books for older children. Shelley was going to become the editor who saw this book through from start to finish. Although both women seemed to believe that I had it in me to go on being a writer, they also agreed that my manuscript needed major structural changes.

Previously I had found writing the first draft of a book difficult. What if you wrote two hundred pages and discovered it wasn't a book at all? Rewriting, for me, had been less tense. Enjoyable even. Now, however, the first draft of each chapter went relatively smoothly, with me dictating, rewinding, listening and polishing. What daunted me was the thought of having to restructure not one manuscript, but three dozen cassettes lined up in a shoebox.

"I don't think that four-year-old sister adds anything positive to this story," Shelley said. "I'd delete her entirely."

Ellen also wanted me to dispense with poor Caroline. Once I'd calmed down, I knew that they were right. But I was filled with dismay when I thought about actually doing this. "Get your hands washed for supper, girls," Melly Talbot kept saying. Caroline popped up in every other paragraph. I groaned and started over.

I trusted Shelley. Her excitement and her ruthlessness reminded me of my father's. He had brought me up to value the editing process. I'd been revising things since the age of eleven.

That fall I went to see the specialist again. He was blunt. The blisters would get worse. When I tried, though, to make him give me some idea of exactly when I could expect to go completely blind, he refused to do so. He did explain why my vision came and went as it did. I was suffering from corneal edema. Sometimes there was more cloudy fluid in my cornea, sometimes less.

The doctor's curt home truths plunged me back into depression temporarily. I'd never get my book rewritten, not with blisters and migraines. Nobody should expect it of me. Despair hates to give up.

When I went to Five Oaks in October for the third time that year, M. T. took me aside.

"You should get a Seeing Eye dog," she said.

"But I'm not totally blind. I'm sure you have to have lost all your sight before they let you have one," I told her gloomily. "It's the one thing I am looking forward to about blindness — having one of those dogs."

M. T. ignored my tone of voice. She simply went on talking about her friends with guide dogs. They were busy, productive, joyous people. "Look into it," she insisted.

As I left, she came out the door especially to repeat this advice. At home again, I began talking about the possibility. It still seemed distant, unreal. But Mother could at least start reading me books about people with such Wonder Dogs.

The blisters began coming every day. At last the doctor prescribed a soft plastic contact lens. It would act as a bandage, protecting the surface of my cornea from my eyelid rubbing against it. The pain at once lessened.

What was more startling, my vision improved. I still had heavily fogged-in hours, but not whole days any longer. My eye still hurt, but for shorter periods.

For a year, Mother and I occasionally talked about guide dogs. During that time, I rewrote my manuscript. And I had Mother read aloud to me book after book about and by blind people.

One snowy day, I decided it was time to stop talking. "I'm going to write and ask about guide dogs," I told Mother.

"Fine," she said.

I had read a lot about The Seeing Eye in Morristown, New Jersey. It was the oldest guide dog school in North America. It seemed to me to be more positive than the others. It demanded a little more of the blind people. And it did not say "for the blind" anywhere in its name. I did not like the condescension implied in that small word "for."

In January 1982, I filled out an application and mailed it in. I was frightened by the very thought — not of the dogs, but of the blind people and the training. What if I flunked? What if I couldn't fit in? I had deliberately steered clear of the blind ever since childhood.

But it was too late. My application was in the mail.

⚞ 15 ⚟

I see thee better — in the Dark—
I do not need a Light—
The Love of Thee — a Prism be—
Excelling Violet—
    Emily Dickinson

That spring, while I waited to hear from The Seeing
Eye, I went to England for three weeks with Pat and
my niece Maggie. Our holiday left me feeling muddled.
When you cannot see sights, sightseeing loses much
of its appeal.

"I'd like to take you and your mother out to lunch
at Grandma Lee's," Aunt Gretta said the morning I got
back. "It'll be a celebration. My treat."

Lunching out was a treat, but only for her. I was
tired and I didn't want to waste time eating downtown
when there was so much to do at home. "Not today,"
I protested.

"Oh, come on. It'll be a Welcome Home party," Aunt
Gretta insisted.

"But I didn't want to come home," I grumbled.

Aunt Gretta wisely ignored this. Feeling manipu-
lated and cross, I gave in. The three of us had no sooner
settled down with our food when Mother glanced up
at two newcomers and said in a delighted voice, "Oh,
Jean, here comes Lillian Gardner with Jenny Stephens,
that English girl I told you about. She came for lunch
one Sunday while you were away."

I looked without favour at the lanky young woman in the heavy coat whom Lillian was bringing over. What I did not need, the moment I arrived home, was to find out that my mother had taken some unknown girl under her wing. The space under there, reserved for lame ducks, was never without one or more bedraggled tenants. And whenever my mother made some lonely soul welcome, I had to be nice, too. I was not feeling the slightest bit nice.

"Jean, this is Jenny Stephens," Lillian introduced us. The warmth in her voice was a rebuke to me. I put down my egg-salad sandwich and forced a smile.

"Hi," I said. "How are you liking Guelph?"

It was an inane question, one I myself hated being asked.

The girl gave me a cool glance.

"Guelph's fine," she said.

She was no more excited about meeting me than I was about being introduced to her. I liked people who refused to gush on cue. She also had not addressed me in either the overly sweet or loudly bracing tone so many strangers used upon first meeting a blind lady who wrote children's books. Maybe she was interesting after all. Perhaps Mother had actually made her welcome not because she felt sorry for her, but because she liked her. I really smiled.

"I was in England just yesterday," I informed her.

"I know," said the young woman, now sounding almost curt.

As they turned to go to their table, I wondered what ailed her. It did not cross my mind until much later that she was homesick.

Later that day I asked Mother to tell me about Jenny again. She was a plant physiologist who worked in the horticulture department of the University of Guelph. She was also on her way to becoming a lay preacher in the British Methodist Church. It did not sound promising. I knew next to nothing about plants and only slightly more about Methodists. The Wesleys had invented them, Grandma had been one and they loved singing. That was all.

That Sunday night, Jenny attended the Bible study group to which Mother and I belonged. Before the evening was out, she had made three ridiculous puns and had not hesitated to argue with the minister. She had also laughed every time I made a joke. She was clearly a woman of discernment. I decided I did like her after all.

But I was preoccupied with wondering whether I would be accepted at The Seeing Eye. Before leaving for England, I had had a medical, found people willing to write letters of reference and filled out a long questionnaire explaining why I wanted a guide dog and what I expected our life together to be like. I tried to be honest, even though I worried about telling them that I spent a large part of my days sitting at a desk in my own home. Should I try to sound more athletic?

For the first time in my life, I feared I would prove to have too much vision. I still saw the blue of the sky, the yellow of the house across the street, the white snow. But I did not see oncoming traffic. Or notice steps up and down, especially inside buildings.

I kept wondering what breed of dog I'd get, what her name would be, how well I'd manage during the training. I even planned our first walk. We'd go to the library.

My family grew sick of the subject. Even Posy, my Maltese, and Missy, who lived with me when Anne

Reuber was teaching, took to yawning loudly when I tried to prepare them.

In April I at last got a letter telling me that I was to be in the August 15th class. The school included a list of exercises and urged me to get in good physical condition before I came to New Jersey.

I went on a diet. And I began walking several miles every day. I even bought a pedometer so that I could keep track. Since I was nervous about crossing large streets, I trudged around and around the blocks close to home.

Mother invited Jenny to dinner again. She walked over.

"Where do you live?" I asked.

"About three blocks away," she said.

If we were friends, I thought, I could walk to her apartment . . .

I believed that though I might become a whiz at Braille, get a guide dog and be a great success as a blind lady, now that I was going blind I would never again make a close friend. Oh, I'd meet new people and they would like my sense of humour and even be eager to know the "real, live writer." But never again would I discover simultaneously with somebody else that we were kindred. How could I when I could not exchange a smiling glance with someone, when I did not even know for certain where people were situated in a room, when I couldn't share a book or play Scrabble or meet someone for lunch?

That June, I was urged to go to the United Church Women "Roots and Wings" conference. I had to find someone to be my roommate and guide, and my other friends were not free. I asked Jenny Stephens if she would like to come.

"I'll think about it," she said.

I wished I had not asked. I didn't really want to go anyway, and plainly she had no wish to accompany me. Jenny called.

"I can go," she said. "Someone will water my plants."

She had not been hesitating to accompany a blind person; she had merely needed to locate a dependable plant-waterer.

Going to "Roots and Wings" with Jenny made me see how foolish I had been when I thought loneliness was an inevitable part of blindness. We not only enjoyed the various meetings during the day, we talked half the night away. As we shared our life stories, discussed our jobs, described our families to each other, I felt that upsurge of joy I had imagined I had lost forever. At three a.m. I turned on the light, fished out an apple I'd been given, sat cross-legged on my bed and bit into it. Jenny, watching from across the room, laughed.

"What's so funny?" I said with my mouth full.

But I knew. We were taking a holiday from sensible adulthood and behaving like twelve-year-olds on a sleepover. I, being fifty, looked especially comic sitting there in my pink pyjamas indulging in a "midnight feast." How I had envied girls in boarding school books who carried on this way! How I had loved this camaraderie at camp and later in residence. How insane I had been to believe that friendships were dependent on eyesight!

Back in Guelph, our comradeship flourished. The fact that we could easily walk the short distance between her apartment and my house helped. We needed each other that spring and summer. She was having problems at work. She was lonely, too, so far from her family and friends. And, as the weeks passed, I was growing more and more nervous about going to The Seeing Eye.

I lost twenty pounds. I walked a minimum of two miles a day. Often I tramped closer to six. I even forced myself to include hills.

And, while doing all that walking, I soon learned just why I needed a guide dog. Even though I carried a white cane and had a little vision, I kept tripping over hoses, running into tricycles, being brought up short by a car parked across the sidewalk. Low-hanging branches smacked me in the face. I skidded on bits of litter. One day I caught my toe in the open end of a lead pipe and measured my length on the cement.

I dreaded most falling over a bicycle. All those sharp spokes and hard pedals and sticking-up handlebars could leave a person seriously injured.

I was delighted not only by how little Jenny seemed to care about the difference in our ages, but how casually she accepted my blindness. Small things that troubled others, she managed so deftly that I was mystified. After all, she had had no previous experience with blind people. I finally asked her how she did one thing.

"When I take a cup of tea from most people," I said, "there's an awkward moment when we try to get synchronized. Yet when you give me one, I reach out and it's there. How do you do it?"

"I wait till you put out your hand before I hand you your cup. They hold out the cup before you reach for it," she said.

It was so simple. But it left me feeling competent and inconspicuous. I loved this quiet thoughtfulness in her.

Another friend, trying to be helpful, plucked my fork from my hand while six of us were dining out in a fine restaurant.

"You've been chasing that bite around your plate for twenty minutes," she said. "I'll just catch it for you."

I sat there, stiff with embarrassment, and waited for her to say, "Open wide!" But she gave me back my fork instead. I ate the bite and then quietly put my fork down. I was no longer hungry. Before she spoke, I had imagined I was eating as competently as anyone, that we were all involved in the table talk, that I was fitting in flawlessly. Her well-meant words had turned me into a sideshow.

That summer, Jenny read aloud to me. We went on picnics and saw plays at the Stratford Festival. We talked for hours and laughed immoderately. One afternoon when we were with another friend, I said something and then turned.

"You stop smiling like that, Jenny Stephens," I ordered.

"You can't see her. How do you know she's smiling?" our other friend challenged.

It was not something I could explain. "I can hear her smile," I said.

If I had not been so tense about going to The Seeing Eye, those days would have been sheer joy. I tried to express their healing in a poem.

> Your friendship is not music, light or food.
> It is instead a buoyant, sheltering ark,
> Warm and alight, which found me in the dark
> And brought me out of desperation's flood.
>
> An ark of rescue. Yet far more than that.
> It is the dove that flutters from my hand

And brings me back a green twig from the land.
And it is coming home to Ararat.

It holds out more than refuge, snug and warm.
It is tomorrow beckoning, the start
Of hope, of joy that springs up in my heart.
It is the blessed bow that ends the storm.

I changed my mind about the route of my first walk with this dog I was soon to get. She and I would go straight to Jenny's.

August came at last. Mother and Hugh and I drove down to New Jersey. As we pulled into the curving drive, I felt like a seven-year-old about to be sick. I didn't know how to talk to blind people. I was going to fail for sure. I wanted Hugh to take me away.

I am fifty, I told myself sternly. I am a famous children's writer. I am just as good a blind lady as any of them.

I got out of the car. We found someone who showed Mother and me to my room. It was like a room in any other residence, with two of everything. There was, however, no reading light over the bed.

Mother hugged me goodbye. She knew I was scared silly.

"Good luck. See you on September 9th," she said huskily.

I waved to the disappearing car and returned to my room. I'd unpack. All these blind people I was about to meet would have "a place for everything and everything in its place."

When I opened the bottom drawer of the dresser, I was momentarily puzzled to find, waiting in it, a square of carpet. It looked like a sample. Then I understood. My dog must be going to use this as a bed.

The dream moved one step closer to reality.

"Miss Little?" a male voice inquired.

I spun around. A man was standing in the open doorway.

"Yes," I said, doing my best to sound as calm as a cucumber.

"I'm Jim Trevasano," he said. "Mr T., they call me. I'm to be your instructor. Would you like to go on a tour of the place?"

"Sure," I said, stepping forward to take his arm.

He held out an empty harness instead. He kept hold of the front part and placed my left hand on the handle.

"Let's go," he said.

❧ 16 ❧

To my small Hearth His fire came—
And all my House aglow
Did fan and rock, with sudden light—
Emily Dickinson

I tried to walk smoothly, to take the corners with ease, to breathe evenly and to get the layout of the place into my head, all at one and the same time. To myself, I seemed to be doing marvellously, but Mr T. said nothing. Down the main hallway we sped. Then he glanced down at my hand and came to an abrupt stop.

"Loosen your grip," he told me, detaching and repositioning my hand. I felt the stiff leather-covered handle settle comfortably into the crook of my fingers. My thumb barely touched it now.

We were off again. I yearned for a word of reassurance.

"This is the Eustace Lounge," he said instead.

What did that mean, exactly? He did not explain. Clearly he had a lot to attend to. He was not impatient, just busy.

Grow up, I told myself. You're doing fine. Relax!

We went up stairs and down, stopping at the head of each flight the way my dog would. He said things but, although I did try, I took in very little. Then we were back at my room.

"When will my roommate arrive?" I asked as he turned to go.

"I think she's coming tomorrow," he said. "She's a

143

last-minute replacement for somebody who cancelled."

"Is she getting her first dog?"

"No," he said. "Her second, I believe. She's from out west."

He disappeared before I could learn more. I sat on my bed and hoped other students would make their presence known.

Then Jo, from across the hall, came to my door and introduced herself. She was getting her fourth dog.

"I'll be so glad to get it," she said with a laugh. "The other day I crossed a street with my cane, and when I got to the far side, I automatically said, 'Good girl!' I felt like such an idiot. But praising them becomes so automatic."

I laughed. She was certainly friendly. All I had to do was give the others a chance. I ventured out of my room and met more of my class. We chatted. I could hear myself sounding self-confident, amused, mature. Well, I was used to faking it.

Until now, however, I'd never had to put on my performance of well-adjusted blind lady for blind people. It was a strain.

"Have you any vision?" they asked me.

Every time I said "Yes," I felt guilty. Did they resent my getting a guide dog while I still had some sight? They must.

Certain customs at The Seeing Eye increased my nervousness. We were expected to call our instructors by their surnames. This might have made sense in the past, yet the habit seemed dated and unnatural now.

There were a good many rules, a rigid schedule, a lot to take in. And we were expected to run the washer and dryer ourselves. Ridiculous as it seems, I spent a lot of time stewing about operating that washer and dryer.

How independent handicapped people are is almost always measured by how much of their own cooking, cleaning and shopping they do. It doesn't matter whether or not you can write a book. It doesn't matter that half the able-bodied people in the world have others to cook, shop and clean for them. You are judged by your survival skills, not by your other talents. People like myself, who can work a computer but who do not do the laundry, find this irritating. It is as annoying as being told, "Blind people are wonderful knitters," or "But you have extra-sensitive touch and hearing, don't you, to compensate for your lack of sight?"

The Seeing Eye's policy is, however, to assume that students can manage the skills of daily living. The staff helps in unobtrusive, tactful ways and, if you are brave enough to avail yourself of the opportunities they provide, you may learn to do many things you previously depended on others to do for you. Some students arrive in Morristown never having been allowed to cut up their own meat or choose which clothes to wear.

I watched some people increase markedly in self-confidence while others hung back, refusing to attempt anything new. I tried to be one of the brave ones, but I was enormously grateful when, later on, my kind-hearted roommate did the laundry for us both.

"It's going to be hard to sleep on Saturday night," Jo said at supper.

It was. We were to be given our dogs the following day.

We discussed, at length, the advantages of one breed over another. Those who had already had a dog were the experts, of course, though I did notice that those who preferred German shepherds had had good ones while those who voted for retrievers knew them best. I worried lest I be given a Dobermann or a boxer. I was not frightened of either, but I had decided I wanted a floppy-eared dog.

"Miss Little, what breed of dog would you like?" Mr T. said casually, as though he had read my thoughts.

"A golden retriever."

"There's only one and he's spoken for," he told me. "We have a lot of shepherds."

"I have two friends who are terrified of shepherds," I said.

"Is this dog for you or your friends?" Mr T. inquired coolly.

"Oh, I'll take anything," I hastened to say, feeling as though I had failed the first test. "I'm so glad to be getting a dog."

In the morning, Mr T. took me for my Juno walk. I had to use the commands and hand signals while he walked ahead of me, carrying the front half of the harness. I held the handle loosely this time and did not require correcting.

We came to the first curb. He stopped and waited.

"Good girl, Juno!" I enthused, feeling like an idiot, but determined to put lots of warmth into my voice.

We went through this ritual at every curb we came to, and Mr T. reminded me to praise him whenever I forgot.

"Sound excited about it," he said.

At the end of the walk, he asked me to demonstrate how strongly I could jerk back on the leash. I jerked with so much force that it pulled out of his hand.

"My, my!" he said, admiration in his voice.

Although later I was to regret showing off that way, at the time I was pleased with my display of prowess.

We were at lunch when the great announcement came.

"Well, we'll be bringing your dogs to you about two o'clock this afternoon," Mr T. said.

We were expecting this, yet a gasp went up from everyone sitting there, old-timers and newcomers alike. I experienced a hodge-podge of contradictory feelings simultaneously: apprehension, curiosity, relief, delight, panic and wild excitement. "Can you tell us what we're getting?" someone asked.

"I'd rather not," Mr T. said. "Some of you have your minds made up as to the breed or sex you want. But we know these dogs, and by now we know each of you a little. We'll do our best to match every one of you with the right dog. If I told you ahead of time, some of you would be disappointed in your dog before you've even met. Trust us and give the dogs a chance. Wait in your rooms. We'll bring them to you as soon as we've given them all a bath."

Under cover of the table, I checked my Braille watch. It was a couple of minutes to one. I had been waiting for almost eight months. As I pushed back my chair, I did not know how I was going to live through another sixty minutes.

I sat on my bed and stared at the empty bed that awaited the arrival of my roommate. I had been told a little more about her. Her name was Peggy Woodward and she was coming from Colorado. It would have been nice to have company while I waited but, on the other hand, it would be lovely to be alone with my dog.

I was sure the dog would be a female. In the books

I had read, all the women had been given bitches. I had decided that if I hated her name, I would change it to Lucy or Nell. Such an intelligent dog would soon adjust. Lucy meant "light," and Nell "bright friend" according to the name book I had consulted. I checked my watch again. At least half an hour must have passed. It was seven minutes after one.

My door was open. I heard Amy and Jo talking across the hall. Unable to bear the suspense alone, I joined them. Jo was getting her fourth dog and, although she was as excited as Amy and I were, she was not at all apprehensive. Both Amy and I admitted that we were terrified. What if our dogs didn't like us? What if the course proved too difficult?

I sat on the foot of Amy's bed, right next to the door. When there were gaps in our conversation, I could hear other people pacing, drifting from room to room, chatting. Nobody was having a nap. Voices were high-pitched, laughter shrill and explosive.

"We're like fathers in the waiting room of a maternity floor," I said.

Although I meant it as a joke, that was exactly what we were like. After all, these dogs were going to change things for us in a big way. We would have to live together more closely than any two people except Siamese twins. Where we went, they would go; when we rested, they would be beside us. If we couldn't get along, there was misery ahead for both of us.

Jo was tolerant with us and comforting. But she reminded us that our routines were going to change and so were the dogs'. They would have to adapt themselves to our working hours. We would have to see that they were fed, given water to drink, exercised and groomed regularly. We would have to keep up their obedience training and take them to the vet. We would have to trot them out at least four times a day so they could eliminate waste and, when they did it in style, we were going to have to pick up after them and tell them how clever they were.

Amy and I grew even more tense. Was it going to be worth it? Had we made a terrible mistake?

Then, all at once, we heard two sets of footsteps coming down the hall. One belonged to a trainer, the other to a dog. Whose was it?

She was a black Lab, her name was Lady, and she belonged to Jo.

"Hi, little Lady," Jo crooned.

Amy and I could no longer talk to each other. We were far too keyed-up. Then her dog, Lark, another black Lab, arrived. I went back across the hall to wait by myself. I heard Barbara and Lucille get their dogs, Opal and Huck.

Everybody was getting her dog except me. Trying to appear relaxed, I began taping a letter to Jenny. I did not sound calm.

Suddenly, Mr T. was at my door. There was a scramble of paws, and an enormous creamy-coloured dog galloped into the room.

"He's a yellow Lab and his name's Zephyr," Mr T. said.

I couldn't believe it. He was so beautiful, the most beautiful dog I had ever seen. He was exactly the kind of dog I had meant when I asked for a golden.

And I couldn't name him Lucy. He was a he!

But I didn't have long to study his conformation. He dashed up to me, hauling Mr T. along in his wake. He swiped his big wet tongue across half of my cheek and all of my left ear. His tail was wagging a mile a minute.

"Anything you want to know?" Mr T. asked.

I shook my head. I hardly noticed his leaving. I was too busy hugging this huge dog.

Zephyr! What a wonderful name!

"Good boy, Zephyr," I told him. "You're so big! I never thought you'd be so big. And you're beautiful!"

He began to whimper. Why had Mr T. left him with this stranger? Then he leaped up, landing on the bed with both front paws.

"Down, Zephyr," I said, determined to be the perfect mistress. "You know better than that."

He did, too. He hopped down and looked penitent for a fleeting moment. In case his feelings were hurt, I slid onto the floor and sat beside him. He went on bouncing around me excitedly for awhile longer, licking my cheeks and my nose. Then, with a big sigh, he folded up, put his head on my lap and went sound asleep.

"You big silly," I murmured. "Don't worry. You'll get to love me. I love you already. Oh, Zephyr, you don't know it, but you're going to spend the rest of your life with me."

I smoothed his velvety ear. My eyes stung. The long wait was over. My Seeing Eye dog and I had started on our life together.

ᴤ 17 ᴤ

I never hear the word "escape"
Without a quicker blood,
A sudden expectation,
A flying attitude!
    Emily Dickinson

My first afternoon with Zephyr was wonderful and incredibly wearing. I began it delighted that my roommate had still not arrived. It would give Zephyr and me time to make friends without anyone butting in. But after two hours alone with him, I was not so sure.

We were to keep our dogs with us every moment of the day. Zephyr would rest beneath my chair while I ate, sleep on the square of carpet next to my bed, escort me to the lounge or the telephone booth. He would even supervise my bath. We would walk the Morristown streets side by side, play together, even go shopping. And I would take him out at regular intervals for Park time.

As a child, I had dreamed of having a dog who would follow me everywhere. I had been certain such closeness would be heaven. The small pet dogs I had had since I grew up had often trailed after me, and I had found this flattering and endearing. Before coming to Morristown, I had thought having a full-time shadow would be a wish come true. Not only would this Wonder Dog worship me; he would obey me. I had tried to train my pets to follow orders, but one and all had barked when I said "Quiet!", fetched when it suited them and asked "Why?" when I said "Come." A guide dog would leap to do my bidding. A guide dog would be a walking miracle.

So I had thought until I met Zephyr. He was not quite what I had expected. To begin with, he seemed outsize. Missy and Posy curled up in small contented heaps when they weren't wanted and faded into the background. This big fellow would never fade.

After an hour, I wanted a nap. Yet Zephyr didn't settle.

Well, he would just have to learn. I stretched out and shut my eyes. He propped his heavy chin on the edge of the bed. I peeped. He was gazing at me with reproachful eyes.

"We're resting, dog," I told him, yawning so that he would get the message. "Aren't you tired?"

No. I'm not. I dozed off five minutes after we met, remember? Naptime is over. Let's *do* something. Let's have a little action.

With some notable exceptions, I dislike books in which animals chat. I am most averse to those in which beasts converse with humans. In the masterpieces of Beatrix Potter, E. B. White and Richard Adams, the creatures talk to each other but waste few words on people. Talking animals make me squirm.

Pets do, however, communicate with their owners. Missy, for one, could remind you sharply that it was her mealtime or express marked impatience when you were slow in putting on her leash. But once her needs were met, she hushed.

Before meeting Zephyr, I avoided putting words into the mouths of animals. That was anthropomorphizing and it was impertinent.

But Zephyr is a talker. While he has not, in my hearing, spoken the English language, he makes it perfectly plain that he understands it. And he uses his ears, tail, eyebrows, various rumbles and grumbles, the slant of his head, a nudge from his huge paw, a thrust of his great, cold nose or a succession of heartrending sighs to get his meaning across.

He also is adept at letting you know when you have finally gotten his drift. He grows ecstatic, "pours on the praise" as my instructors would say, and through the adroit use of flattery and persistence, invariably succeeds in getting his own way.

If I were to keep saying in this account, "He seemed to be saying . . ." or "He appeared to want . . .", I would be belittling his powers of speech.

To give one example, he will begin perhaps by staring fixedly at the top of the wardrobe where I've hidden a rawhide bone. If I pretend not to notice, he races back and forth until I am forced to glare at him. The instant my attention is caught, he snaps back into his fixed staring stance. If I still refuse to look, he lopes over and leans on me. I can't ignore seventy-five pounds of solid dog. "Get off me, you lummox," I yell. Aha! Now he's got me. He gallops noisily back to his starting point. He bangs his tail against whatever will make a noise. Whack, whack, slappity, bang! I may grit my teeth, but he knows I'm weakening. I will give in because he will not give up. This is a dog deserving of respect.

He does not just talk about dog biscuits or rawhide bones, either. When he thinks I've been talking long enough, he grunts, They've had it. Listen to that Velcro rip. Finish off fast.

Oh, he talks. And he wants answers. If I don't

respond, he repeats himself — loudly. If there's an audience, he hams it up. If they laugh, he gives them an encore.

That first afternoon, I was unprepared. I made up my mind to be firm. "Naptime," I repeated. It took him three minutes to bully me into getting up and taking him on in a spot of wrestling. When we were both out of breath, I tried again to snooze. The instant my eyes closed, he yanked his leash out of my limp hand, raced to the door, put his nose to the crack and started to howl.

Drat him.

Jo and Amy and their dogs were just across the hall. Lucille and Barbara and theirs were next door. Although I had heard the clicking of paws and the murmur of loving voices, I had not once heard any other dog yowling.

I retrieved him and scratched behind his floppy ears. He rested against me, half closed his eyes and gave a sigh of rapture. I had an ominous presentiment that despite all the time I had spent getting myself in shape, this seventeen-month-old dog was going to be more than a match for his fifty-year-old mistress.

At four-thirty, they brought me a pan of food to give to him. He leaped and larked around me, not lunging to get it but simply celebrating its arrival. When I put his dish on the floor, he dropped down onto his stomach, wrapped his front paws around the bowl and polished off its contents in seconds. I watched in amazement. Never, in all my years of being a dog owner, had I come across one who took food lying down.

I next offered him water. He lapped a little, his tail wagging happily, but he could not keep his mind on it. Something was happening in the hall.

"Park time," Mr T.'s voice called.

We did not have harnesses for our animals yet. We had been told to "heel them" down the hall. Down the hall we trooped, dogs hauling instead of heeling. Well, maybe some were walking correctly at heel. Mine certainly wasn't.

At The Seeing Eye, taking dogs out to park means taking them outside to a large paved area where they can relieve themselves. You do this immediately after you have fed them at five-thirty in the morning. You go again at ten-thirty, four-thirty in the afternoon and at eight-thirty in the evening. The dogs soon grow used to this schedule and do not ask to be taken out at other times.

That first time, we newcomers felt highly self-conscious as we were directed to positions a few feet apart from each other and began walking our dogs in circles and entreating them to perform.

"Hurry up, boy. Park time!" "Come on, girl. You can do it." "Let's not spend all afternoon here, fellow. Park time. *Park* time!"

The chorus is amusing if your dog is kind enough to cooperate. If everybody else's does his or her business promptly and only you are left, it loses its appeal. The instructors help enormously by remaining good-humoured at such times. That afternoon, I was more relieved than Zephyr when he got the idea almost immediately.

"Good boy, Zeph. Okay, Miss Little, go straight ahead . . ."

I followed Mr T.'s crystal-clear instructions and safely climbed the steps into the building. But Zephyr still did not know what "Heel" meant. He tore down the hall, flying me behind him like the tail on a meteor. He dashed straight to our room.

A stranger was there, unlocking a suitcase that lay on top of the spare bed. My roommate! Zephyr bounced up and down, his tail whipping around in circles. You'd think she was a long-lost friend of his.

"Calm down, boy," I said, but I didn't really blame him. I was excited, too. I introduced myself and my dog.

Peggy straightened up and beamed at us. "Hello, Zephyr," she said, letting him sniff her fingers. "What colour is he?"

"He's blond. A yellow Lab."

"Oh, they are wonderful," she said. "My Florrie was a yellow Lab. I had to have her put to sleep on Thursday . . ."

Her voice cracked.

"How old was she?" I asked quickly.

"Only six," Peggy said. She had control of herself again. She explained that Florrie had developed an incurable kidney disease. Then we changed the subject.

Whenever I lost heart in the next two weeks, Peggy cheered me up with tales of her own early doubts and of how perfect her relationship with Florrie had become.

Then her instructor arrived with Fancy, her German shepherd.

If Zephyr had been excited on meeting Peggy, it was nothing to his instant infatuation with Fancy. Knowing that Peggy should be left alone with her new dog, I removed him and myself to the nearby lounge. It was not a dignified exit. I told him to heel, but he utterly ignored me. I had to drag him away by brute force.

Lucille and Barbara and I sat and chatted. Our dogs

amazed me by settling down next to our chairs just as we had been told they would. I smiled at Zeph, so well behaved all of a sudden, and then looked at the other two dogs. I could not see either one. Whereas Zephyr stood out plainly because he was such a pale colour, Huck and Opal, both black Labs, were invisible. I was grateful to the staff at The Seeing Eye for choosing such a light dog for me. Since I still had some vision, I could enjoy him much better because of his high visibility. I could not see him in detail as a fully sighted person could, but I could tell which way he was facing, what he was doing and, to some extent, see his expression. One of his most endearing ways was to tip his head over sideways when he really wanted something. I could tell, if he were close to me, when he was trying this on.

When we went in to supper, all twenty dogs settled down under the table with only a little reminding. Everyone who was there for the first time was astonished by how well they tolerated each other. The returnees assured us that this was normal. They enjoyed explaining things. Although, a day or two later, we would all sound like experts, that night we humbly drank in every tip.

We had a meeting after dinner. We were to put our dogs into harness the next morning. We went over the commands we would have to use on our first walk. The instructors explained what we were to do if the dogs became distracted or failed to stop at a curb.

Back in our room, Peggy and I talked at length about our past lives. She was dumbfounded to find herself rooming with a published writer. I was just as impressed on discovering that she had been a ranch cook for years. She had other disabilities besides her blindness.

She was very deaf and wore hearing aids in both ears. She had had an arthritic hip replaced and wore an orthopaedic shoe because one of her legs was shorter than the other.

As I listened, I soon realized that in spite of these problems and although she was older than I, Peggy was far more fit. She swam every day and travelled around America competing in Senior Olympic swimming meets. She'd won medals.

"Heavens," I said, feeling feeble just listening to her.

My roommate Peggy, her dog Fancy, Zephyr and I.

The following morning, Mr Roberts came to collect Barbara, Lucille and myself. I was surprised.

"I thought Mr T. was my instructor," I said.

"It's a large class," Doug Roberts said comfortably.

"I'll be working with you three instead."

We three were considerably older than most of the class. I suspected, although I never got Mr Roberts to confirm this, that they thought we might be slow learners and need extra coaching. But I felt at ease immediately with this new man.

He loaded the three of us and Zeph, Huck and Opal into the van, and we headed for Maple Avenue, the Seeing Eye's nursery route. Mr Roberts took Barbara and Lucille first. I sat alone in the van, stroking Zephyr's soft ears and trying to relax. The others were gone a long time. Then, there they were, laughing, talking.

"Praise your dogs," Mr Roberts reminded them as they started climbing back into the van. "Tell them they did well."

"How about us?" Barbara asked, but his reply was muffled by a scramble of paws, excited panting and swishing tails.

"All right, Miss Little. Your turn next," Doug Roberts said.

He sounded as though he was positive that Zephyr and I would do beautifully. I gulped and clambered awkwardly out onto the walk. We were on a quiet side street that cut across Maple Avenue.

"Bring him alongside of you. That's it. Relax, Miss Little."

He checked to see that I was holding the leash threaded through my fingers properly and that my hand was curled around but not clutching the handle. I had it right. I felt very slightly smug.

"Fine. Now go straight ahead to the corner," Mr Roberts said as he fell back a pace.

I took a shaking breath and cleared my throat.

"Zephyr, forward," I said. The husky voice speaking those words sounded like a stranger's.

Then Zephyr obeyed. Without stopping to stare up at me, he went calmly and competently ahead and, tugging me after him, led the way to the corner. When he reached the curb, he stopped. So did I. He glanced up at me inquiringly. He was actually waiting for me to tell him what to do next. He believed in me.

"Cross here and, when you get to the corner opposite, turn right," Mr Roberts told me. "And don't forget to praise him."

"Good boy, Zephyr," I said hastily. "Good boy!"

But I spoke automatically. I was still dazed by the wonder of what had just happened. It had been so long since I had swung down any street at that pace. My life, limited by my blindness and timidity, underwent an enormous change in that moment. I knew I had a long way to go. I was still afraid I would flunk the course. Yet I felt heady with freedom, filled to the brim with a singing joy. I had escaped forever from having to depend on well-meaning people. I wouldn't have to wait, have to ask, have to hang on, have to be grateful any longer. This marvellous dog and I could go anywhere we chose — on our own.

The route we took seemed incredibly complicated, the commands difficult. It was not till a couple of afternoons later that it dawned on me that all the turns we had made had been right turns, and that the complex route consisted mainly of going around a simple rectangle. The street was peaceful. There were no challenges from Zephyr's point of view. Yet I doubt that I have ever felt a greater sense of accomplishment than I did when my dog and I made it safely back to the van where Barbara and Lucille waited.

"You're a good match," Mr Roberts told me and my guide dog. "That was a good trip. Now pour on the praise, Miss Little."

I did so, unaware that in those few minutes, I had learned the most important lesson — to trust my dog. That trust was to waver once in awhile, for Zephyr and I were still inexperienced, still not a team. Yet all my life I will remember that magic moment when I said "Forward" and he went. And the second, just as wonderful, when he came to the curb and stopped, without my saying a word.

❧ 18 ❧

I started Early — Took my Dog—
And visited the Sea—
The Mermaids in the Basement
Came out to look at me—
        Emily Dickinson

The weeks I was about to spend training with Zephyr were more for my benefit than his. I had everything to learn. He only had to come to realize that I had replaced his trainer as the person for whom he used his intelligence, to whom he gave his heart.

It wasn't easy for him to make this transfer. He had had to move too many times before. Like a foster child meeting yet another set of parents, he was wary at first. He was never hostile or unfriendly. But he would not allow me to be special.

Some blind people are disappointed when they fail to get instant adoration from their dogs. But I did not want a dog who showed no lasting loyalty to the people whom he had previously thought of as his. If he had loved me on sight, it would have meant that he would be happy to leave me, too, and move on to someone else. I did not want a fickle Seeing Eye dog.

I was pleased by the fact that Labs have a reputation for friendliness. A possessive, single-hearted "one-woman dog" was not what I needed. The two of us would visit schools and libraries, travel in planes and on trains, attend conferences held in large hotels, go to the theatre and to church. A dog who resented everyone but me would be a great worry in such social situations.

I did hope, of course, that some day soon he would show me that he regarded me as his central responsibility, his important person, but I reminded myself that he was seventeen months old when we met. He had memories and experiences I had not shared. We would have to take time getting to know each other.

I did my best to find out what had happened to him during that first year and a half. He had been born on March 15, 1981, in The Seeing Eye kennels. He had had a brother and sister to tumble about with and a kindly mother to teach him all a new pup needs to know.

There had been people there, people who brought food and water, who liked dogs, who were always in a hurry but who still spoke to him and the other pups in friendship. These humans were kind, but no one was special to him. They were mostly just gentle hands and voices.

He had no notion that his future had already been decided. He was examined by a veterinarian. He was startled when he was given shots, but he soon forgot. He was x-rayed and his ear was tattooed.

Then had come the upsetting day when he had been removed from his family and taken to live full-time with strangers. At first he had been homesick for the kennels. But the people, particularly one young one, petted him and played with him and laughed at his puppy ways. They had soon made him feel that their farm, with all its room to run and its fascinating smells and its unkennel-like comforts, was his real home. He adopted the family as his own and forgot he had not lived with them always.

Although everyone on the farm seemed fond of him, he saw that he meant something special to one of the children. Zephyr did not know that this particular child was a member of 4H and was taking part in their Puppy-Raising Project. He knew only that this one young person spent extra hours playing with him, grooming him, feeding him and teaching him manners. This child became the centre of his world.

I wish I knew more about this family. The Seeing Eye, unlike most other dog guide schools, does not give its students information about the families who have looked after their dogs during their first year of life. The reason for this is not given. Even when I said I would settle for learning merely the sex and age of the child who raised him, since it would make this part of his story so much more vivid for the reader, they would or could not give me the answers.

I do know, though, that these people did a marvellous job. Not all guide-dog owners are given a dog who hardly ever barks, who never chews up anything that does not belong to him, who has only three times forgotten that peeing inside somebody's house is the height of wickedness and who trusts and enjoys people as much as Zephyr does.

Guide dogs are amazing, but they are still animals. I have known a guide dog to snatch food off the table. I have met one who speedily became overprotective and is a worry when strangers come around. I have met one who barks loud and long when anyone goes down the hall outside the apartment in which he lives. I have met a couple who beg shamelessly. And I know one who cannot be taken to a concert because whenever she hears music, the dog also bursts into song.

I am grateful that Zephyr's 4H family had strength

enough to teach him civilized behaviour. It is hard to be consistently firm with a lovable puppy who does his best to cajole you into breaking every rule in the book. That family's good sense during the months he spent with them makes living with him today a pleasure.

The only food he has ever stolen has been down on a coffee table. He claims that he genuinely believed it to be a table meant for dogs. He only barks when someone rings our doorbell and none of us hears. When he does bark, he does it only once and then hangs his head in shame. He doesn't beg by whining or pawing. Mind you, he does stare at every bite going into a person's mouth, and he drools. I, of course, am blind to such blackmail. "Zephyr, stop begging!" people have commanded. I hate other people ordering my dog around. Besides, if a cat can look at a king, surely a Seeing Eye dog can gaze at a mere commoner eating.

Although the family who raised Zephyr all knew he was going to become a guide dog, Zeph himself had no inkling of this. He was unprepared when the day came for him to be returned to the kennel so that he could begin his secondary education.

Giving the dog back must be heartbreaking for everyone involved. Yet what happens to the pup during that first year is crucial. Guide dogs, to be any good, must be highly responsive to their blind owners and must assume responsibility for them even when they are unable to give appropriate commands. A dog who is largely indifferent when it comes to people is absolutely worthless as a Seeing Eye dog. They must be loved so that they in turn will be loving. They must acquire a sense of purpose by being taken seriously from the beginning. They must be encouraged to think.

Zephyr must have been bewildered the day he was

returned to the kennel. He must have expected the child he loved to come any minute to fetch him. But days passed and his family did not appear. Instead he played with other dogs and was subjected to further tests. He is a happy-hearted dog. But he missed hearing one loving voice telling him what a good boy he was, one particular pair of young hands taking time to pat and groom only him.

And then, at last, along came a new person called Kathy Waite. She said all those delightful things, took time to scratch the right places, played with him, was indisputably his. He basked in the lovely attention but waited and watched to see whether she would also forsake him. But, like most Labs, he found it impossible to hold out for long. He liked people so much. And, when she made it plain that she thought him a dear, he could not resist her blandishments.

He did notice that she gave equal time to other dogs. He strongly disapproved of this. But after awhile he was so sure that he was her special pet that he was able to tolerate her occasional lapses.

Then one day she slid a stout leather harness over his head, buckled it under his chest, took the handle in her hand and told him how handsome he looked. He twisted his head around to see what she was up to. He definitely was not in favour of the thing, whatever it was. He did his best to get it off.

"Easy, Zeph," she soothed him. "You look great. Good boy."

He calmed down and even gave her a tail wag, but he was still confused. She held onto part of the harness and urged him to walk along.

"*Good* boy, Zeph!" she enthused when he took one step.

He was a sucker for a bit of blarney. If she liked him so much in this crazy get-up, it seemed a small price to pay. He no sooner figured out just how to march along to please her, when she took him out on the street.

He was walking along confidently, stepping down off the curb as any sensible dog would, when she had a fit of some kind. Yank went the leash, half choking him.

"Phooey! Phooey!" she yelled.

She was mad at him. That was crystal-clear. But why? He had not put a paw wrong.

She backed him up. Off they went again. Thank goodness she had come to her senses. He stepped unhesitatingly off the same curb.

"Phooey! Bad boy. Phooey, Zephyr." Yank, jerk, ouch!

What on earth was the matter with her? He was mystified. Back they went. Were they never going to get past this bit of sidewalk? He trotted along more slowly now. Here came the curb where she lost her mind. Seeing it coming, he hesitated for a split second.

"Good boy! *Good* boy, Zeph." She was ecstatic. Well, whatever had been wrong seemed to be over. He sighed with relief.

"Forward," she said.

Fine. That meant he was at last going to get a proper walk. He did not even notice the curb ahead until she went into her mad fit there, too. It took quite a few curbs before he had it figured out. When he stopped, she was happy. When he kept going like a sensible dog, she was furious. Well, he liked her to be happy. If stopping at curbs would do it, he would stop at curbs.

Three months later he had heard hundreds of

"Phooeys" and "Atta boys." He now knew lots of other things that pleased her or drove her wild. He had to watch out for oncoming cars. He had to take her around hydrants, parking meters and tree trunks. He had to take her through turnstyles. He had to stop for steps.

The most difficult task she required of him was watching out that nothing smacked her on the head. She *really* got upset whenever the smallest leaf brushed against so much as one hair. He could not think why she couldn't keep an eye out for such things herself. Her head, after all, was closer to overhanging branches than his. Even so, he began looking up.

He even learned how to please her when they rode on elevators. He was to go straight to the back, turn and stand quietly. When they came to down stairways, first she wanted warning and then she liked him to go down slowly, steadily, almost sedately. She never made allowances, not when he had that harness on. When she said, "Zephyr, straight!" it meant stop veering over to have a look at something in the gutter. He had never dreamed she could be so fussy.

But he loved her with all his big soft heart. She had a way of saying his name that made him bounce with joy. She adored him.

Then she disappeared out of his life, and I came into it. I knew where to scratch and I said, "Good boy, Zeph." I was just as pleased as Kathy when he stopped for curbs. He quite liked me.

But I was not his person.

On our second training trip, he spotted Kathy half a block away. Tail wagging furiously, he began to dash towards her.

"Give him a leash correction, Miss Little," Mr

Roberts said sharply. "He sees Kathy Waite. That's what is distracting him."

I jerked hard on the leash.

"Phooey! Bad boy!" I reprimanded my dog.

But my heart wasn't in it. Perhaps he knew that. He went right on trying to get to Kathy.

"Hold onto him and wait," Mr Roberts commanded. "We'll let her get by. Then we'll go the other way. Keep him at 'Sit.' "

I was looking down at him while we waited. Slowly his tail stopped wagging at top speed. His ears, which had humped up in excitement, flattened. The bliss that had set him quivering drained out of him as he watched his idol departing. He could see she had another dog with her. He did not notice that somebody else was actually holding that dog's harness. He looked dejected, heartbroken even.

I told myself not to be silly, but I felt like a dog-napper — not only stealing a pup but doing it callously within sight of its owner. My heart ached for him as he stared sorrowfully after Kathy.

"I'm sorry, boy," I murmured quickly as Mr Roberts took a moment to speak to another instructor.

Zeph was deaf to this. If I were really sorry, I'd have let him go. My grip on his leash showed just how sorry I was.

Later on, Kathy brought the feed pans. She came right up to the door where Zephyr and I waited. Once again, when he recognized her he went wild with delight. He danced about, his tail whamming the door-jamb. At last, at long last, she had come for him.

Ignoring the delirious dog at my side, Mrs Waite handed me the pan of food. It was hard for her, but he did not know that. When she turned away, without once speaking his name, he stared after her in shocked bewilderment.

"Come and get it, Zephyr," I coaxed, waving the dog chow under his nose. Even though he loved to eat, my dog wouldn't come at first. He went on staring down the hall.

At Park time, there was Mrs Waite again, supervising eliminations. Certain that she loved him, positive that out here in the bright sunlight she would be sure to recognize him, Zeph lunged in her direction. I held on for dear life. Why did he have to be so powerful? Kathy walked past. She deliberately did not so much as glance down.

Zeph could not believe it. What was the matter with her? I yanked on the leash and, moving automatically, he came. But he was confused and hurt. He must have done something terrible, but he had no idea what.

"Park time, Zehyr," I reminded him, piloting him around me in a rough circle. "Park time, boy."

Head down, he plodded around me. He looked like an old dog.

Dogs are faithful creatures, but most of them are also resilient. Although he went on yearning for Kathy to notice him, to pardon him for whatever he had done to offend her, Zeph made the best of things when she was out of his sight.

But he wasn't about to give his heart away again. He was not going to trust another human only to find her faithless, too. He would be polite but keep his distance.

In the meantime, he did his best to teach me everything he had learned. The hardest lesson for me was to pay strict attention to what he was trying to tell me. I would start chatting with the instructor or thinking about what was happening to my manuscript, and I would not even notice that he had stopped moving forward. I would take one more step and lose my footing as the sidewalk ended abruptly and I landed awkwardly in the gutter. I would start to scold him but would realize that he was standing still at the curb exactly the way he was supposed to.

I was too slow giving leash corrections. Mr Roberts told me to speed up and showed me yet again how to do it properly. I determined that the next time Zephyr erred, I'd give him such a swift, sharp correction that Mr Roberts would be dumbfounded.

Zeph, all at once, did a peculiar little sideways hop. Slam! The leash jerked back.

"PHOOEY!" I yelled.

Zephyr accepted the mighty rebuke and led me on. At the next corner, Mr Roberts came up beside me. He was chortling.

"Would you like to know what really went on back there?" he asked.

Annoyed at him for being amused instead of praising me for doing so well, I said, "What?"

"A lady came towards you pushing a baby in a go-cart," he said, still chuckling. "Just as you got close, the baby hauled off and pitched its plastic bottle, full of milk, at the poor dog. It got him right between the eyes. A direct hit. Poor Zephyr jumped. And you lammed into him just as I had told you to do."

I was filled with repentance.

"Oh, poor Zeph. I'm sorry," I began to apologize.

Mr Roberts told me to cross the street and turn left.

"Don't worry about it," he called after me. "He's forgiven you already. And he knows he shouldn't hop about like that. But it was a comical sight."

As we walked on, I realized that such misunder-standings must be part of a guide dog's daily life. Their blind owners must often misinterpret their actions and scold them for things that aren't their fault. But the pride the dogs take in their work, the praise they are given, must make up for an occasional misplaced "Phooey."

As our first week together passed, Zephyr and I really did begin to work as a team. Each day I felt closer to him. He was friendly in return, but I saw no clear sign that he was beginning to consider me as his very own. I kept hoping he would wag differently for me some day, but he seemed equally happy to see Peggy or Barbara or Amy.

Then Peggy and I went to church, leaving our dogs in the kennels. Maybe Peggy took in the sermon. I stewed about Zephyr, left behind, feeling abandoned. I could hardly wait to get back.

Mr Roberts brought our dogs back to us. He released them at the far end of the hall. Both Fancy and Zeph-yr flew down the passage, barrelled into our room and flung themselves upon us. Now Zeph was not even glancing Peggy's way, and Fancy was ignoring me. Their relief and rapture when they found us both sit-ting there waiting for them was plain. They had not liked being back in that kennel. They had wanted us! I had never in my life seen a dog as jubilant as Zephyr was at that reunion.

"Well," Mr Roberts said with a grin, "they certainly know who they belong to. What excitement!"

I had been reluctant to leave my dog but now, as I gave him a hug and got a wet lick on the ear, I was so glad I had gone. My dog really knew he was mine — and he was happy about it at last.

"Don't you worry, boy," I promised him, giving him yet another hug. "Next week you'll go to church with me. And if I ever do leave you again, I'll always come back."

☙ 19 ☙

The feet of people walking home
With gayer sandals go—
Emily Dickinson

I enjoyed my trips with Zephyr through the streets of Morristown. I liked chatting with Peggy, too, about her years as a ranch cook. Yet I found the three weeks at the school an interminable stretch of time. Much as I needed the training, I longed for the day when I would have Zephyr to myself.

Becoming a student again at fifty wasn't easy. My self-confidence grew steadily under Mr Roberts' capable instruction, though. I stopped believing I would flunk and decided it was time to pay for my dog.

Although the cost of training a Seeing Eye dog runs into the thousands, students coming to the school pay a mere $150 for their first dog and only $50 for replacement dogs. Paying this modest sum makes the dog yours in a way he would not be if he were simply handed to you. Students are encouraged to earn this money themselves. Nobody is refused a dog because he or she cannot find the cash. Students may go home with their dogs and later pay a bit each month.

By now Zephyr no longer seemed outsized. All the dogs at the school were big. No Pomeranians make it at The Seeing Eye. After all, if a dog has to yank his blind mistress out of the way of a speeding car, he has to be sizeable enough for her to notice what he's up to.

Over and over again in the years ahead, people would look at my yellow Lab and say, "But I thought guide dogs were all German shepherds!" I now knew better. Many different breeds have been used successfully. Although there were only German shepherds, yellow and black Labs and one golden retriever in our class, I had by this time heard of Dalmatians, boxers, short-haired collies and crossbreeds who worked well as guide dogs. The breed is not important. The health, intelligence and temperament of the dog are what matter. Seeing Eye dogs must be eager to please, as well as being calm, patient and smart enough to learn the difference between such commands as Left, Right, Forward, Sit, Rest, Come, Down and Fetch.

Hup-up is another important command which depends, for its meaning, on when it is said. It usually means "Move it" or "Hurry up." Occasionally it means "Quit stopping three feet back from the curb." "Inside" means take me into this building, and "Outside" means take me back out the way we came in. "Find a chair" means exactly what it says — plus the understood word, "unoccupied."

Zephyr had mastered all of these commands before we met. Even while we were at The Seeing Eye, I could tell that he was adding new words and phrases to his vocabulary. Not yet. That's enough. Go to bed. I'll give you to the count of six. One . . . Two . . . Dinner.

It was exhilarating to have a dog who knew so much. During the first few days, I had been amazed again and again when he quietly did exactly what I told him to do. My several pet dogs had always thought long and hard before obeying any orders of mine that didn't suit them. They gave in like grumpy children; Zephyr cooperated like a colleague.

One day Zephyr and I came to a street controlled by traffic lights. I listened, trying to sort out the traffic sounds. Zephyr stood waiting for the word "Forward." He was unable to judge by the colour of the light since he, like all dogs, is colour blind and unable to tell red and green apart. When I thought all the cars passing in front of us had halted and I could hear those on my right beginning to move, I gave him the command, "Forward." Usually the moment I said this, he stepped smartly down off the curb and piloted me across the street. This time he did not stir. My right foot had begun to move, but I jerked it back and hoped Mr Roberts had not noticed. How many million times had he reminded me, "Trust your dog, Miss Little. He can see; you can't. Never ever step out in front of him." I was puzzled, though. Nothing was coming. "Forward, boy," I repeated firmly — just as a stealthy bicycle whizzed past. Zephyr did not glance up, but I knew what he was thinking.

"What a very good boy!" I said humbly.

"This morning," said Mr T. the next day, "we're taking all of you to the train station."

I could tell that this was some kind of test, but I was not prepared for the moment when he lined five of us up across the rear of the platform, explained that ahead of us lay a drop-off of a couple of feet, and then told us to give the command, "Forward."

Nobody rushed to speak the word. What if our dogs had forgotten all they had learned and our instructors realized this a moment too late? We'd plunge face-down onto railroad tracks.

"Forward," said a reluctant chorus.

Our dogs marched confidently across to the drop-off point. Then, without any fuss, they made a right turn and blocked our way.

"Good boy!" "Atta girl!" everyone sang out thankfully.

"Try going around them," Mr T. called.

I stepped further to my right. Zephyr promptly moved to prevent me from taking one forward step. I shoved against him, attempting to go left. He stood his ground and would not let me.

Then, dizzy with relief, we went for a train ride. My dog lay quietly tucked under the seat and seemed to enjoy the outing.

Every day, Mr Roberts kept an eye out for distractions that would take Zephyr's attention off his job. I thought he wanted me to have more practice making leash corrections. But Zeph was now concentrating so well that I could not understand the trainer's concern. After all, I knew how to handle dogs. I had taken my West Highland terrier to obedience classes, and I had owned three other dogs since. I had never gotten them to obey as well as Zephyr did, but I knew exactly how to reinforce the fine job Kathy Waite had done with him. Other people might have problems after they went home, but I was sure I wouldn't.

It was obvious to all that some of our number had more trouble with their dogs than others. We spent a good deal of time gossiping about each other's progress. I was sure one or two would require an instructor to visit them at home. How humiliating for them!

"Get ready to give him a leash correction, Miss Little," Mr Roberts said. "We are about to pass some squirrels. He's already looking in their direction."

I got ready. So did Mr Roberts. But Zephyr faced front and marched by the squirrels without a glance. Mr Roberts sighed.

"Why not simply admit Zephyr's wonderful?" I asked jauntily. "Why try to lead him into temptation?"

"He may change his ways after you leave," my instructor said. "You have to know how to handle him if he does get distracted."

I could not imagine a day when I would not be able to manage my paragon of a guide dog.

The routes we took got harder. My migraines didn't help. I also had the corneal blisters to contend with. They made my eye inflamed and fogged me in. Nobody else seemed to have vision that got better and worse every few hours. One minute I would be able to help a blind classmate find something she had lost. An hour later I would see nothing but white mist.

Then, one evening when we had the dogs out for Park time, a young dog escaped from his trainer and came bounding down to the paved area where we were grouped. Its trainer called and it circled around us and went running back towards him. But not before Zephyr had risen on his hind legs and given a great, booming bark.

I was flabbergasted but, by now, I knew enough to correct him. Yet I was still too slow. Mr T. sprang at him, grabbed his collar, catching one of my fingers in its metal links, and whammed him back to the ground. He then gave him a violent shake and roared a fusillade of "Phooeys" at him.

Sucking my mangled finger, I stood and watched my dog being given the scolding of his life.

What a fuss over nothing! I thought. I was even a little proud of my dog's huge, ear-shattering bark. I had never heard it before.

It never crossed my mind that this was not an

isolated occurrence — that it was, instead, a portent of real trouble ahead.

Peggy and Fancy left at the end of two-and-a-half weeks. Both Zeph and I missed them a lot, but we were busy practising going through revolving doors, coming down a spiral staircase, going to a nearby mall to shop.

I began, during those final days, to count the hours till I could have my guide dog to myself. But on the very last evening, something wonderful happened. I had told Kathy Waite that I did not want a dog who was faithless and that I felt Zephyr was still bewildered and hurt by her apparent rejection of him. So, when we were sitting in our empty room, she came to say goodbye.

Zeph looked up at her and moved his tail a little, certain she would not speak to him. When she said, "Hi, Zephyr," he leaped up, unable to believe it. She picked up the lacrosse ball I had bought him and hid it behind her back. He charged around her and jumped to get it. She stayed for nearly twenty minutes. When she left, he sank down next to me with a deep, blissful sigh.

He had seen me pack his grooming things and his extra dish. He knew he was coming with me, that we were a team. But it was all right. Whatever he had done could not have been so terrible. Kathy Waite had forgiven him at last.

"We're going home tomorrow, Zeph," I said softly, leaning down to fondle his velvet ears.

Thump went his tail. Slurp went his tongue across my chin. He did not look at the door. He looked at our suitcase instead. He knew I needed him. Wherever I was going, he was coming along.

That last night, I scarcely slept. Butterflies jigged and

reeled inside me. I was not frightened; I was simply too keyed up to settle. I made it worse by playing over in my mind the scene of the two of us, Zephyr and I, walking all on our own through the gate at the airport. And Mother would be standing there, probably having to blink back the tears when she beheld with her own eyes my friend and the independence he had given me.

Janet would be there, too. She was making a special trip to meet this princely guide dog who was now entirely mine. It was going to be a perfect moment, the kind you dream of having but rarely achieve. If only morning would come!

I had several surprises in store.

The first was a plump, elderly woman who got onto the plane just after Mr T. had settled us in our seat and waved goodbye. I had never before been on a plane where the seats faced each other. When the woman saw she was to sit directly across from the large dog, already peacefully asleep at my feet, she let out a shriek.

"I can't sit there," she shrilled. "I'm allergic to dogs — and I can't eat bananas, either."

She was plainly in a panic. The attendant led her away.

Throughout our training, we had been warned that we would encounter people who for one reason or another would object to our dogs, but the people of Morristown are so understanding that I had imagined it was something that happened rarely and only to other people. I spoke reassuringly to Zephyr, who was still sound asleep and had no idea he had been insulted.

Then another plump, elderly woman was shown to

the seat. She pulled back in alarm. "I don't want to sit anywhere near that dog," she declared. "I don't trust dogs. I've been *bitten*."

"He's very gentle," I pleaded. "He'd never bite you."

"He'll stay gentle till he wakes up and sees me," she said.

The flight attendant, frazzled, asked if she would really mind. Her adult children, sitting across the aisle, were laughing at her. Turning a deaf ear, she lowered herself into the seat.

Zeph slept. I hoped for the best. The woman ignored her gleeful offspring and waited for my attack dog to raise his head and grab a piece of her ankle. As we neared Buffalo, though, she grew calmer. When Zephyr, still sleeping, stretched out one of his front paws and I dove down to snatch it back, she said in a quiet, slightly sheepish voice, "Leave him be. He's not doing any harm."

It was my first, but far from my last, experience of Zephyr's power to disarm. He can transform an enemy into a friend, a friend into a slave. He can cast spells with the help of his eyelashes, his tail and his melting gaze.

When we landed in Toronto at last, the flight attendant told me to wait till everyone else had gotten off. Then the agent would come to "deplane" me. I objected. This was why I had gone to get a guide dog. Zephyr would follow the other passengers, and I was being met. I did not need help.

The flight attendant blocked my way to the aisle and became frantic. I must wait. I really must. I gave in. When the agent arrived, I would explain.

But the agent was worse than the flight attendant. When I told her I did not need any help, she assured me that it was no bother. She would just see me to whoever was meeting me.

"Well, you go ahead then," I told her, "and he'll follow you."

She did not trust us. Twice she darted back and clutched at my arm when she saw an obstacle in our path or some unevenness underfoot. Both times, since I was unprepared for her shove, I half stumbled. She looked smug.

Then she told me we were coming to a flight of stairs.

"He'll stop to show me where they are," I said, pausing to talk to her face to face so that she would hear. "Please, don't take hold of me. He's been trained to follow. Walk ahead, please."

"I'm only trying to assist you, madam," she said sulkily. She then began to stride ahead in offended dignity. I breathed a sigh of relief. Zephyr followed her. But as we reached the head of the stairs, she dodged back and, grabbing hold of his harness, wrenched him to a stop far too early. I was outraged. So was Zephyr.

"Don't touch his harness again," I blazed. I was furious at her not only because she was interfering, but because she was ruining the independent arrival I had been picturing for days. How could I get rid of her?

Just before we reached the spot where I would be met, I stopped dead in my tracks. I had already told her that I had a little vision.

"Oh, there they are, the people who are meeting me," I said. "Thanks for your help. I can manage fine by myself now."

She hesitated. This was not according to her plan.

"Are you quite sure?"

"Yes," I ground out through gritted teeth. "Goodbye."

She had no choice but to take herself off. Zephyr and I stood stock-still until we were certain she had gone. Then we moved forward side by side, the way I had planned. But even though Mother and Janet were waiting and said all the right things, that insensitive woman had robbed both Zeph and myself of the joyous serenity I had counted on feeling.

When we got home and he had explored the house and eaten his first meal and gone out for Park time, Zephyr and I walked over to Jenny's. When we came home again an hour later, we were accosted by a golden retriever. It came up, sniffed at Zeph, stared at me and departed. While it was giving him the once-over, my Seeing Eye dog ignored it completely. He just plodded steadily along as if the two of us were alone, as if he had not even noticed the golden.

"Good boy!" I enthused. "Good, *good* boy! What a wonderful dog!"

And, as I heaped on the praise, I marvelled at the training he had had. I had never before seen any dog show such self-control. Kathy Waite and all the rest of the instructors at the school had achieved the impossible.

⚘ 20 ⚘

My Portion is Defeat — today—
Emily Dickinson

I was grooming Zephyr a month or so later when his choke-chain collar slid over his head, fell to the floor and became a straight length of chain with rings at either end. I picked it up and stared at it. There was a trick to putting it back on, something you did to keep it collar-shaped. They had shown us how at The Seeing Eye, and I knew, anyway, from taking Susie to obedience school.

I turned the chain over. What you did was simple. I could figure it out. An expert like myself would not need to ask.

Finally I clipped the two rings together with the snap on his leash. I knew in my heart that that was not right, but it would work, wouldn't it?

"Is Zeph's collar on properly?" Jenny asked.

"Yes," I snapped.

She did not persist. I, after all, was the one who had gone to Morristown to be educated. And Zephyr was doing his work flawlessly. I took him to the theatre, to church, to a corn roast, to a conference. Everybody was impressed.

"Yes, he is wonderful," I kept saying.

But within six weeks, I knew something was wrong. My wonderful dog was no longer ignoring other dogs. The moment he spotted one, even in the far distance,

Jenny and I with Zephyr.

his breathing quickened and he strained forward, trying to reach it. He pulled so hard that I had trouble controlling him. He seemed unaware of the sharp leash corrections I gave, deaf to my cries of "Phooey! Bad boy!"

At first he only pulled and panted.

If I'm really strict, he'll soon stop, I told myself. He can't have forgotten his training. Any day now I'll get through to him.

Yet the situation got steadily worse. His hackles began bristling. If we got close enough, he even reared up on his hind legs and barked ferociously.

He was a model guide dog in every other way. He

found me a chair. He lay quietly beside me while I lectured. He enjoyed seeing *The Tempest* at the Stratford Festival. He ignored passing cats or squirrels or pigeons. When people admired him, I smiled and prayed they would go before he saw a dog coming and went berserk.

I should have phoned The Seeing Eye at once and asked for help, but I couldn't admit defeat. Obstinately, I went on trying to do what I had been taught. I gave him millions of leash corrections. The first two or three times it happened on any given outing, I could silence him and get safely past whatever was causing the rumpus. After that he was too strong and too stubborn for me to make any lasting impression on him.

Whenever we were engaged in a battle of wills, I felt the whole world was watching. Many a passerby was only too happy to advise me or to admonish Zephyr. I started plotting our routes down streets that had fewer dogs. I soon found that Guelph had hordes of canines on every block — all outside and off their leashes.

At the end of October, I went to Five Oaks to attend another Medical Mission Sister weekend with M. T. Although my struggles with Zephyr had already begun, I was still excited about showing him off. Miriam Therese had been the first person to suggest I go to Morristown. When Jenny and Zephyr and I walked in, he upstaged us completely, but I was used to that by now. I felt such an enormous difference in myself. The last time I had been there, I had been in the grip of a bleak despondency that darkened the entire world. Now I was teaching children's literature at the university, writing and in the company of this beautiful, intelligent creature who obeyed my every command.

Well, almost my every command.

Early Saturday morning, I took Zephyr out for Park time and met M. T. on her way to breakfast. We stopped to greet each other when, all at once, a smallish, inoffensive dog ambled by at a distance. I did not see him, of course, and so was unprepared when my highly educated dog lunged, his hackles up, and gave voice to a great growl. I went into action, but it was several minutes before I wrestled him to a stand-still. I heard someone say, "Oh, no!" as I yelled at my dog and did my best to jerk his head off.

"She has to be tough," M. T. said sharply. "Keep out of it. She knows what she's doing."

Her vote of confidence was like balm to my wound-ed self-respect. When I had dragged Zeph back to the doorway of the main building, and the other dog had meandered out of sight, I had to face a cluster of on-lookers who laughed and told me how shocked they were to see a Seeing Eye dog misbehave like that. I could not join in their banter. I was ashamed of their seeing my tussle with Zeph. I was shaking, and I had all I could do to keep back tears.

It wasn't funny; it was frightening. My faith in Zephyr rested on his proven co-operation and good sense. Now he was failing me, and I felt helpless and betrayed.

M. T. did not laugh. Neither did she add any teas-ing remark to those I had just endured. She did not say anything to me about it until after lunch when she could see I had recovered my equilibrium. Then she got me off by myself.

"Jean, call The Seeing Eye," she said. She came from Morristown, she reminded me, and she knew what she was talking about. "They can help you. That's what they're there for. They'll send a trainer or tell you what to do. Let them know right away."

"I guess I should," I muttered miserably. "But . . . maybe he'll straighten out yet. If I'm just firm enough."

She shook her head. "Phone them as soon as you get home," she insisted. "You won't be the first. Didn't they tell you to keep in touch?"

They had. But I did not promise to call them.

I put it off till the winter day Zephyr saw a poodle looking out the back window of a passing car. The car was heading out of Guelph down a major highway. Five streets met right there. We were ringed by heavy traffic. My marvellous dog did not hesitate. He simply charged after that car, dragging me along willy-nilly.

Car horns honked. Brakes squealed. I tried to dig in my feet, but my boots skidded in the slush churned up by passing wheels. At last I managed, using every ounce of strength I possessed, to haul him to a standstill. Then, half crying and hurling invective at him, I towed my rebellious guide to the nearest curb.

As I crouched over him there, trying to catch my breath and fighting against breaking down and howling, one passerby laughingly told me what had gotten him so distraught.

"It must have weighed all of ten pounds," he reported.

"You don't need to be so harsh with him," a whippet of a girl scolded. "Just speak firmly and he'll understand. Violence only frightens animals."

I answered neither of them. I had meant to go on downtown. I about-faced and made for home, where I could cry buckets without anyone commenting. As Zeph, quiet and biddable now, took me back across the same street, another spectator muttered, loudly enough for me to hear, "That dog's vicious. He ought to be destroyed."

When I got home, I didn't stop long enough to take off my wet boots or Zephyr's harness. With him watching me, puzzled but patient, I dialed the number of The Seeing Eye.

They were so understanding and supportive that I wished I had called weeks before. I had hoped to talk to Mr Roberts. I spoke instead to Mr Boeke. I was in awe of him because of things I had heard people say while I was at the school, but he could not have been kinder. He told me several things to try.

He was shocked when I confessed that I did not know how to make Zephyr's choke chain work properly, but he told me exactly what to do. It was so simple. What a fool I'd been!

"No wonder you've been having trouble," he remarked.

"I don't know how I could have been so stupid," I said.

He could have gone on about it but he didn't. Probably he could hear the tears in my voice.

The Seeing Eye staff frequently get calls like mine, especially from first-time guide-dog owners. These dogs are young and sometimes headstrong. Their owners hesitate to be as firm as they should. They hate to keep scolding such beloved animals. They don't take seriously the warnings they are given at the school.

Occasionally a dog is not suitable for guiding and, even after being given to another master or mistress, proves intractable. Sometimes the person simply does not have it in her to discipline a dog as one must. Once in awhile, dog and student turn out to be incompatible.

Seeing Eye trouble-shooters know all of this, but they do not let their impatience or their doubts show.

Over the next few months, I tried all their suggestions. I smacked him with a rolled-up magazine. I put a muzzle on him each time he was bad. I yanked him around and I yelled at him. And I kept hoping he would ignore other dogs so I could pour on the praise.

The only problem was that he refused to oblige. It was as though he had gone past the point where he could get the message. I could stop him, make him sit and lie down, berate him. But the very next time a large dog crossed our path, he went for it.

In May, Peggy and Fancy came to visit. When we went to meet them, there were two gates through which they might come.

"Stand here," Mother said to me. "I'll go to the other gate. That way we won't miss her."

I obeyed until an official came along and started shooing us all back. I stood my ground.

"I'm meeting a blind lady with her Seeing Eye dog," I told him. "I have to stay here or I'll miss them."

He stared at me. Then he scratched his head.

"Is she blind?" he asked.

I nodded.

"Can you see?"

I shook my head.

"But if you can't see her and she can't see you, how are you going to know . . .?"

I smiled. "Oh, the dogs will know each other," I told him. "They roomed together at school."

He went away and, a moment later, returned leading Mother. He took us through one gate to a spot where the hall divided. He sat me on a stool. From there we could see Peggy before she had to turn left or right. While we waited, we heard him talking to a pal.

"Now I've heard everything," he said. "One blind lady meeting another blind lady — but the dogs will know each other."

They did. Such excitement!

But that evening, when we took them for a walk, Zephyr saw a dog across the street and went into his act. Peggy, who had been giving me lots of sage advice, was shocked. He would not stop even when she shook him long and hard. Fancy watched wide-eyed.

"Phone The Seeing Eye," she said. "That is terrible. I've never seen anything like it."

I phoned the next day. I talked to Dick Krokus. He said Zephyr sounded incorrigible. They'd give me another dog. I began to cry.

"But he's so good in every other way," I wailed. "If only he could be made to stop this . . ."

"Do you want me to send somebody up there?" he asked. "We could try a last-ditch attempt, if you want. I'm pretty sure it won't work. What do you say?"

"Yes, please," I sniffled.

He cleared his own throat.

"I'll send Dan Boeke," he said. There was a pause. Then he spoke gently for such a gruff man.

"Keep your chin up, Miss Little," he said.

✺ 21 ✺

The Vane a little to the East—
Scares Muslin Souls — away—
. . . Broadcloth Hearts are firmer—
Than those of Organdy—
Emily Dickinson

After I hung up, Peggy kept on and on about how bad Zeph was. I must confess that when her model dog Fancy snitched an entire loaf of bread off our dining-room table, I was pleased as punch.

Mr Boeke came a couple of weeks later. When the doorbell rang, Zephyr, innocent and eager to welcome whoever had come to call, ran ahead of me to the door.

I felt as though I had told my child we were on our way to the circus when I was really taking him to the dentist. I steeled myself against weakness. Feeling sorry for him would not help. I knew he loved me. Now I had to love him enough to do whatever was necessary to enable him to work well again.

The person standing on our front step was a combination of wizard, angel and drill-sergeant, but he didn't look like it. I couldn't see him clearly, of course, and I was too nervous to be taking mental notes on his appearance, but I did register that this man's appearance was not extraordinary in any way.

"Miss Little?" he said, extending a firm, steady hand. "I'm Daniel Boeke."

"Hi," I said, trying to sound calm and failing utterly.

As Zephyr pushed up to sniff at this guest, Mr Boeke told me that he would not pay attention to the dog yet, not till he'd seen me work with him after lunch.

"They're smart," he said, stepping into our hall. "They seem to sense when a trainer is around and then they shape up. I don't want him to guess till I've watched him in action. He looks good."

He added then, in a faintly surprised voice, "He really looks good. I thought he'd be fleshed out."

Score one for me and Zephyr! I might have made many mistakes, but I had not overfed him. I had kept him exercised, too. I could tell Zephyr's good health was a point in my favour. My heart grew lighter.

While we ate, Mother asked Mr Boeke what had made him go to work at The Seeing Eye in the beginning. He told us, in capsule form, his life story. It made fascinating listening. He had been turned down by the school when he inquired about a job training guide dogs. They learned he had had tuberculosis and, even though he was well again, they felt he was not robust enough for what has to be one of the most strenuous jobs going. He had been hired only after applying three times. By now he had been working at training dogs and blind people for thirty-five years. He was about to retire.

I know there are other trainers at The Seeing Eye who could have come to Zephyr's and my aid and perhaps done it equally well. Even so, I am grateful that I didn't wait a couple of months longer before I phoned. This down-to-earth, serious, frank and caring man was the exact person Zephyr and I needed.

The minute we finished eating, Mr Boeke, my

Seeing Eye dog and I set out on a search for big, barking dogs.

"I'll just drop back and watch. You take him wherever you like," my instructor told me. "I'll be watching but pay no attention to where I am."

I walked to Garth Street and turned right. I knew there was a dog there who could be counted upon to bark madly the moment he guessed we were near. My plan worked to perfection.

"Rrrrufff!" it remarked as we neared the end of its driveway.

Zeph braced himself and took a deep breath to give a full-throated reply. I jumped him, doing my level best to execute a fast and powerful over-the-head correction. Then, just as I completed shaking poor Zeph, Mr Boeke materialized at my elbow.

"You're doing fine," he said, "but now let me show you."

He showed me. He showed Zeph, too. My dog knew for sure, before he quit, that he had a real trainer to reckon with.

"Take your time, Miss Little," Mr Boeke said to me. He seemed to repeat everything at least three times in slow, simple sentences. It was exactly what I needed. I wanted to understand what to do differently, and yet I was too tense to take in a glib stream of complicated instructions, too sick at heart over my fear of losing Zephyr to handle a lecture on what a lousy job I was doing. Mr Boeke did not beat around the bush. He did not try to butter me up. He was straightforward and practical. Yet a saving sense of humour gleamed through every so often.

He was marvellously funny as he told me precisely what Zephyr was thinking. It was comical but it rang true. I am positive that man really does know what goes on inside a dog's head.

I had been trying to give the leash correction too quickly, not getting hold of Zephyr's collar properly in my rush to get him stopped before he got started. I had also been too gentle with him. Even though I did not try to spare him, when Mr Boeke did it, Zephyr was yanked right off balance, toppled over backwards and jerked forwards again before he could get himself together. Mr Boeke's "Phooey!" was also impressive — sharp, angry, authoritative and quelling. Zephyr lay down meekly and seemed to have had enough.

I knew that was temporary. I'd seen him chastened before. The docility never lasted long. I told Mr Boeke this.

"Let's go on," he said tersely.

When we got to the park, we met a feisty little dog who yipped at us in a crescendo of fury. I did my best. Then Mr Boeke took over and, as he said himself, "put the fear of God into him."

This time Zephyr showed some spirit. The minute Mr Boeke let up on him and he heard that dog still egging him on, he breathed deeply and went back at it. Mr Boeke first shook all the fight out of him and then shook his head over our chances of breaking such a strong instinct to be aggressive.

"He's a real hard neck, this dog," he said with a sigh. "Did you hear him start to growl again, even after I'd given it to him? Miss Little, this isn't going to be easy. He's a stubborn one. He's tough and you won't be able to hurt him. I couldn't get a yelp out of him. I thought I would, but no! And if I can't make him yelp, you sure as hell can't. This is going to be tough. Don't get your hopes up too high."

I felt a swift satisfaction. I wished Peggy had heard that bit about his not being able to make Zeph yelp. My pleasure was only momentary. My hopes were already high. Something *had* to work.

We went on, the two of us with firmly set jaws, Zephyr glancing anxiously over his shoulder every few steps. We met other dogs. Once Mr Boeke whipped my seventy-five-pound dog right off his feet and whirled him around in an entire circle without so much as a toenail touching the earth. Zephyr was so scared that he urinated in mid-air. When he did come in for a landing, he and I walked past that particular dog four more times while Mr Boeke and its owner stood back and observed.

But the fight had pretty well gone out of Zephyr. You could tell he wanted to growl. He didn't dare.

I remember passing a Samoyed, a black Lab, a couple of terriers, some midget breed I didn't know, another Lab. By suppertime, we had walked six miles and Zeph remembered the lesson from one time to the next. My dying hope sprang to life again.

Teaching him he was being bad in a way that would prevent him from repeating the offense had been the impossible thing. I had been able, with great effort, to stop him each time, but it had never had any carry-over. I thought that if only Mr Boeke could make the dog really understand that he was not supposed to lunge and bark, and do this in such a way that Zephyr could recall this when he was next tempted, I could reinforce the lesson and prevent backsliding. Now I might get a chance to prove whether I was right. I felt excitement stirring within me.

We headed home late in the afternoon. As we walked together, I told Mr Boeke that just in the last ten days, Zephyr had begun refusing to fetch certain things.

"What happens?" Mr Boeke said, sounding delighted by this bit of bad news.

Mr Roberts had explained, long ago, that the obedience exercises such as "Sit," "Rest," "Come" and "Fetch" were our opportunity to remind our dogs that we, not they, were in command. When a blind person is out with her dog, she has to trust his judgement even when she suspects he is pulling a fast one. If he balks and will not go forward, she must assume he has a sound reason for doing so. Otherwise she might find herself falling down a manhole. Yet the dog may be testing his power, choosing his own route, doing what he likes instead of what he's told. During the obedience exercises, the person knows exactly what the dog should do, and she need have no compunction about delivering a sharp leash correction if he challenges her authority.

"From the start," I explained, "Zephyr has always done the obedience exercises well. And he has always loved fetching things."

"But now . . ." prompted Mr Boeke, as though he knew what was coming.

"Well, without rhyme or reason, he suddenly began refusing to bring back certain things. If I throw a rolled-up pair of socks, he races after them and runs right back with them in his mouth. They are like balls, maybe, and he's hoping for a game. But just lately, when I throw my pencil case or one of my sneakers, he goes up to it, looks it over and comes back without troubling to pick it up. I've scolded him and escorted him to the object. Then I've tried placing it in his mouth while I say "Fetch!" sternly. As soon as I release it, though, he lets it plop on the floor. Then he stares into space as though he has no idea what's going on. I know how to make him sit or lie down or stay but not how to make him close his teeth on something if he just won't."

"Good, good," Mr Boeke said, almost rubbing his hands with glee. "We'll soon fix that. A good lesson may make him remember."

Poor Zephyr. He had been unwise to attempt this revolt only a few days before Daniel Boeke came. Mr Boeke knew exactly how to force him to fetch, and he taught me how, too. Zeph tried not picking that pencil case up a couple of times, but he must have regretted it when he ended up having to retrieve it nine times in a row. We had to push his head down, force his jaw open and then, if he failed to close it on the pencil case, just keep pushing it down and not releasing him until he finally gave in.

Compelling him to do this was not easy, and anyone watching without understanding what was at stake would have thought us cruel. Mr Boeke warned me that someone would report me to the Humane Society if I corrected my dog as sternly as I should.

"Don't let it bother you," he advised. "Tell them to get in touch with us if necessary. This dog loves you and wants to stay with you, but right now he can't understand that if he doesn't shape up, you'll have to send him away. Remember that his happiness is at stake, not just yours."

After that day, I never had to force Zephyr to retrieve anything again, and his old pride in this skill returned fullfold.

My teacher went on to say something endearing and unexpected.

"You tell him all about it, Miss Little," he said. "He might not understand the words, but tell him anyway. Explain to him that you love him and want to keep him, but you'll have to give him away if he goes on being bad. We can't know what dogs are thinking, but they're smart and they sense things. He wants to please you. I can teach you to correct him, but whether it will work depends on the love bond between you. You've got to put the fear of God into him with those 'Phooeys' and that magazine. You've got to yank him back so hard that he won't forget it the next time. But you also have to show him you love him and pour on the praise when he's good. And sit down and talk it all over with him."

At the end of the day, Mr Boeke summed up everything for me once more and then said, "He's big, too big for you really. He was such a marshmallow during training that we thought there wouldn't be any problems. I thought before I watched you with him that there was no hope. But I've changed my mind. Now I think you have about a twenty-percent chance. I didn't know before how strong you were, how much you want to keep him and how much he loves you. Sometimes people just say, 'Take the dog back. He's no good and I can't be bothered.' But you are going to give it all you've got, I can see that. If it doesn't work, don't worry. We'll give you another dog and he can go to a strong man. He's a powerful dog, that's certain. But he knows now what he's been doing wrong. He'll probably toe the line for a couple of weeks and then he'll test you. Be ready for him. You just might be able to make the lesson stick. When he comes in from a good trip, give him a cookie and tell him he's great. There's hope, Miss Little. Don't be too surprised if . . . well, never mind that. Good luck. Let me know how it works out."

He offered to come back the next day, but we both knew that he had already taught me all I needed — confidence, my anger and that bond of love.

As I stood in the doorway and thanked the rescuer whom The Seeing Eye had sent, Zephyr kept well behind me. He was not so favourably impressed with Mr Daniel Boeke. He devoutly hoped this man, who was up to all his tricks and knew exactly what to do about them, was going for good.

He had no idea that Daniel Boeke was one of the best friends he had.

❧ 22 ❧

And Life steps almost straight.
Emily Dickinson

In bed that night, too tired and too tense to sleep, I went over all the helpful hints Mr Boeke had given me.

Take your time but act fast. Carry the rolled-up magazine always at the ready and let him see it. After smacking his nose with it, drop it and yank him backwards, toppling him right off his feet. Then jerk him forward again before he has time to think straight.

I grinned. I'd make those "Phooeys" in as close an imitation of Mr Boeke's voice as I could.

Best of all, Mr Boeke had said, "When he comes in from a good trip, pour on the praise and give him a cookie." He had only mentioned that at the very end, but I had been wanting to be told something of the sort for a long time. Zephyr's favourite pastime was eating. He associated my feeding him with my love for him. A "cookie" would say "What a marvellous fellow you are!" more memorably than any speech.

Guide dogs are all trained to work simply for love and praise. If you rewarded them with food every time they carried out a command, you would soon have dogs the size of elephants, whose minds were so preoccupied with the next bite that they would be useless as guides. This makes sense and should not be deviated from unless all else fails. In Zephyr's case, all else had. Mr Krokus had said once, "In the last analysis, use the rule W.W. Whatever Works."

Before the pair of us left the house together at nine o'clock the next morning, I gave my guide dog four pieces of dog chow and let him see me put a handful in my pocket. He wanted more. "Phooey," I said and waved a copy of *Maclean's*, rolled into a tight cylinder and done up with rubber bands, in front of him. He looked away.

As we stepped out the door, poor Zeph scanned the nearby bushes for a lurking trainer. Throughout the entire trip, he glanced back frequently. I rejoiced to see him so rattled. I had picked a route liberally sprinkled with canines. "Liberally sprinkled *by* canines, too," I joked to my dog.

Most guide dog owners talk to their dogs as they travel along. It helps focus the dog's attention and expands his vocabulary.

We approached the driveway where Zeph had received his first mighty "Phooey!" from Mr Boeke. A volley of barks sounded from the enemy camp. I braced myself but, although Zephyr turned his head and tensed visibly, he did not dare risk even a marked hesitation. He broke into a near run instead, and passed the danger point at top speed.

"Good, *good* boy!" I was crowing jubilantly. "What a clever, good boy! Fantastic, Zeph! Oh, you are so good!"

I had picked a short block deliberately. I babbled his praises continuously until he pulled to a halt at the curb. Then, to his intense surprise and gratification, I gave him *five* small pieces of Purina. I planned to cut this down to two later, but I was not going to skimp this first morning. I had to make him understand.

"Good, good boy!" I crooned on, sounding fatuous.

Zephyr did not ask any questions. He gobbled down the unexpected treat, licked his chops and looked hopeful.

"Zephyr, forward," I said firmly.

We found a second barking dog less than a block away. I tensed again. Zephyr took a quick look back and then whizzed ahead. Once more, when we reached the corner, a little further away this time, he got his edible reward.

The third time he resisted the urge to bark, he turned expectantly and nosed my pocket.

"Not yet," I said, laughing in spite of myself. "Not till we make it to the corner. Hup-hup, boy. Move it."

He faced front obediently and continued guiding. That third time, once we reached the corner, he was ready and eager for a handout. But he still did not quite get it. When we reached the next curb, even though not a single challenging bark had split the air, he swivelled around and stood, tail wagging, obviously convinced I meant to reward him at the end of every block.

"Phooey. Pay attention," I scolded and straightened him around with my knee. "Zephyr, forward."

Confused but willing, he led me on down the street.

"Woof . . . WOOF!" said an obliging boxer from behind a fence.

Zephyr checked, but only momentarily. Once again, having shown such stellar self-restraint, he got his Purina.

We passed seven dogs during that first trip, without a single eruption of backtalk from mine. I could scarcely believe it. I arrived home beaming. It was too soon to be sure, but my hope now soared like a kite. Both Aunt Gretta and Mother were in the kitchen.

"It worked!" I burst out. "He walked right by dog after dog! He speeded up, but Mr Boeke said he would. I didn't have to correct him even once!"

"I'm so glad you won't have to send him back," Aunt Gretta said. "That would have been a terrible thing to do."

"It isn't settled yet," I snapped. Why did she have to jump the gun like that? If I had to get another dog in order to travel with safety, then I'd have to, terrible or not. I did not need to be told how dreadful it would be.

I was even more excited than she, of course, by the apparent change in Zephyr, but I was afraid to count on it this soon. What if, at the end of a couple of weeks, he went right back to his wicked ways. My hopes had been dashed before. Perhaps he was incorrigible.

But when we went out again after lunch, he was still incredibly good. I did have to give him one energetic leash correction right off the bat, but with only that single reminder, he was a model guide dog the rest of the way.

The next day was good, too, and the next and the next.

Jenny left for a job in Winnipeg a week later. It was hard to say goodbye. Zephyr, with whom she had always had time to play and to whom she never said "Phooey!" would miss her terribly.

"I don't know how we will get along without you," I said, giving her a last hug.

"Let me know about him," she said needlessly.

The first few days in a new place are always difficult. Jenny and I spoke together by phone more often than we should have done, considering the expense. Each time, though, I had good news to tell her. In the days before Mr Boeke came, I had been having at least five or six pitched battles with Zephyr every time I took him out. Now, using my new skill, I could either prevent the trouble by fast talking and quick action, or I could jump on him so hard that he never got the upper hand.

The worst moments came when a dog sprang into view without Zephyr's having any warning. If even a Yorkshire terrier popped out from behind a hedge, my Seeing Eye dog would forget his training and grow momentarily agitated. Taken offguard, he felt we were both menaced, and he overreacted. But I came to understand that if I remained calm, he quickly recovered his aplomb and pretended nothing whatsoever had happened.

The day the two weeks were up, I held my breath. Would I be equal to his testing when he tried it on?

It never came to a real battle. Now when we went out and encountered no dogs, he led me along at a reasonable speed almost always and kept his mind on his work. When a bark did sound, he perked up immediately and, quickening his pace slightly, made for the next corner. When he pulled to a stop, instead of facing forward, eyes on the traffic, he would look up at me happily and begin wagging his tail.

"Yes, you were wonderful," I'd say, smiling back, and I'd fish out a couple of bits of dog chow.

If the menacing dog had been really rude, and my hero had shown himself to be impervious to even the worst insults, he would get three or even, when I was weak, four chunks of chow. It was not the food alone that did the trick, though. It was Mr Boeke's reminding him of his purpose. It was my improved leash corrections. It was Zephyr's beginning at last to heed the blame and work for the praise.

A short time after this reformation, I no longer

needed the magazine and, most of the time, I could even forget the tidbit. He reminded me, when we reached home, of the army of dogs he had valiantly ignored and I would "give him a cookie," but he would be good without it. He had remembered, just in time, that he was a Seeing Eye dog.

Two months after Mr Boeke's visit, however, Zephyr did disobey me. It was early afternoon, and my dog and I were walking through St George's Square in downtown Guelph. We were in the grip of an Ontario heat wave, and I was sorry I had stirred out of my cool house. The heavy, humid air pressed down on the top of my head like a gigantic, meaty hand. I felt bathed in sweat, and I could feel the burning heat of the cement clear through the soles of my sandals.

Poor Zephyr had no shoes to protect his paws. I had been cruel to bring him out on such a horrid, torrid day.

As we plodded past the fountain, I looked longingly at the sparkling fall of cool water. A dog, resting in the slight shade by the bus shelter, saw us and gave a lethargic bark. Zeph took one quick look at the offender but faced forward again without my needing to speak.

"Good boy!" I said, pouring on what praise I could summon up. "Poor dog, I should never have brought you out . . ."

As my words died away, Zephyr turned left.

If it hadn't been so hot, I would have given him one of the magnificient leash corrections Mr Boeke had taught me. Zephyr was not supposed to make a sharp left turn in the middle of a block. He was to execute such an action only after he had stopped for a curb and waited for a command. He might veer to miss an obstacle, of course, but there was no obstacle. And he hadn't veered. He'd made a ninety-degree turn in the middle of a block.

All this flashed through my mind, but I did not correct him. I followed him instead. He couldn't lose me, not in Guelph. Even if he did, I could always ask a sighted person for help. And I was curious. I had to know where he was bound.

A large object loomed up in front of me. Before I registered that it was a city bus, my Seeing Eye dog took me briskly up the high steps.

"Zephyr," I gasped. "Zephyr, wait."

He did not pause. Instead, he towed me to the front seat, plunked himself down next to it and looked up at me.

If you want to walk, lady, that look said, you go right ahead. I, however, am taking this bus.

I gazed back helplessly. I didn't even know what bus it was. It felt empty. The bus to our street did wait somewhere along this stretch of sidewalk, but several bound for other parts of town lined up here, too. Smart as my dog was, I was sure he couldn't read.

The driver climbed on and greeted Zeph like an old buddy.

"I know this sounds crazy," I said, "but could you tell me where this bus is going?"

It was going right past our corner. Out of all the many buses congregating around the square, my Wonder Dog had chosen the one that would carry us home.

☙ 23 ❧

Experiment to me
Is every one I meet
If it contain a Kernel?
The Figure of a Nut

Presents upon a Tree
Equally plausibly
But Meat within, is requisite
To Squirrels and to Me
        Emily Dickinson

The doorbell rang. Zephyr galloped down the hall. He was too well trained to jump up on guests. He simply danced around them, gave an inquisitive sniff and beat out "hallelujahs" with his tail.

"It's Jo Ellen, you numbskull," I said, catching hold of him.

For the past six months, Jo Ellen Bogart and I had driven in to Toronto together to the monthly meetings of CANSCAIP, the national organization for children's authors, illustrators and performers that I had reluctantly helped to found in Port Colborne eight years before. This group, the Canadian Authors Association and the Writers' Union of Canada had introduced me at last to other Canadian children's authors. We also ran into one another at various conferences and literary gatherings. Robert Munsch and Jo Ellen herself were children's writers who actually lived in Guelph.

I had only one fault to find with them. They wrote picture books, not novels.

Now, as we whizzed down the 401, Jo Ellen uttered a sentence that sent my blood pressure sky-rocketing.

"I wrote a book last night," she said.

I had been working on *Mama's Going to Buy You a Mockingbird* for six years, and it was still unfinished. How dared this young upstart say such an outrageous thing in my hearing! I drew in a deep breath. Although I did not speak, Jo Ellen flinched.

"Oh, it's only the text for a little picture book," she said deprecatingly. "It's strange. Sometimes I can't write anything for weeks and then, all at once, three things just come."

I knew about not being able to write for weeks and I, too, had had things just come. But never, ever, an entire book in one evening. It wasn't fair; it wasn't decent. Surely she must be going to spend months polishing. Even so, I hated her.

"What's it about?" I asked coldly.

She told me. It was wonderful. I forgave her instantly. "That is going to be snapped up by the first publisher who sees it," I predicted.

"You really like it?" Jo Ellen said shyly, eagerly. I knew exactly how she was feeling. Most of us, when we first share a new work with someone else, are over-come with doubt, however long we've been writing, however secure our reputation.

"I love it," I repeated. "What's the program tonight?"

"Illustrators," said Jo Ellen.

I sighed. Meetings concerned with the visual arts bored me unless the speakers were as articulate as they were artistic. I attended such meetings because the drive with Jo Ellen and the CANSCAIP crowd let me escape from my continuing spells of depression and my frustration over my book. Also I liked keeping up on the gossip of the children's book world.

We entered the church gym.

"Hi, Zephyr," said Audrey McKim, who had been writing books for children long before I thought of doing so. Belatedly, she added, "Hello, dearie."

As others welcomed my dog, one in three remembered I was with him. I took this for granted by now and didn't begrudge him the attention. Soon he'd have to lie still throughout first a business meeting, then a period when members showed off their new books, records or cassettes, and, finally, the panel. He went to sleep the instant the President called the meeting to order. I listened until the slides began. Then I went to work. Long since, I had learned to compose light verse or work on knotty plot problems while pretending to be spellbound.

". . . thank you for a wonderful program," said the President.

Zephyr and I snapped to attention as we caught those words. I braced myself for the social time that came next. People mingled, gossiped, got coffee, moved on. They all wore name tags, but no name tag was ever large enough to be helpful.

"Hi, Jean," said a voice. "How are you?"

"Fine," I responded bravely. "Who are you?"

"Don't you know? I thought you'd recognize my voice by now."

"Guessing voices isn't one of my parlour tricks," I said, doing my best not to explode.

"Here's your coffee and cookies," Jo Ellen came to my rescue.

"Thanks," I said. "No, dog. They aren't yours; they're mine."

My rescuer vanished. Zephyr sat directly in front of me, staring fixedly at my food. Everybody told me this.

"The poor thing's *starving*." "How can you resist those big brown eyes?" "Doesn't he get even one bite?" "Poor Zephyr!"

"He is not hungry; he is just greedy," I said. "He's had a biscuit. He knows he doesn't eat when people do."

"May I just give him this tiny shortbread?" cooed someone.

"No. Please, don't," I answered.

His leash jerked. Hot coffee splashed over my hand. I heard my dog's jaws snap shut on the cookie she had tossed him.

"I asked you not to do that," I growled.

"I know, but those big eyes are irresistible," she gushed. "I'm a real dog lover. I can't be held responsible."

"I love him enough to want him to live a long, healthy life," I began and then stopped. She had melted into the mob. What was the use? She didn't care that Zephyr had to go into restaurants and bakeries, attend receptions and barbecues. If he gazed expectantly at the food in people's hands, he and I, not she, would be blamed.

As I fought down my anger, I knew I shouldn't be wanting to punch somebody merely because she gave my dog a cookie. What was the matter with me?

I knew. I felt blind.

I scalded my tongue on the coffee and ate my short-bread too fast. Then I stood alone, trying to pick a friend's laugh out of the hubbub and doing my best

to appear happy, involved, anything but abandoned.
I heard no known voice.

So move, I snapped at myself. Find a conversation
you can join in on. Don't hover and quiver like a big
baby. I stepped towards two shadows deep in talk. I
felt the same wretched tension I had known at age ten
when it was my turn to "run in" at skipping.

"So I said enough was enough and he'd have to
leave," said one of the voices. "I can't take any more."

I backed away hastily and trod on Zephyr's paw.

"Sorry, boy," I murmured. Then I leaned down and
started talking to him in earnest. "Zephyr, these people
are not friendly and I wish we'd stayed home. How
about you?"

Such plunges into *sotto voce* conversation had
puzzled my guide dog at first, but now he knew his
part. Wag, wag, wiggle, wag. This time, though, he
listened for only a moment. Then he set out to find
me a friend. I followed, liking our purposeful air. He
stopped by someone and gazed up at her intently.

"What can I do for you, dog?" asked an unmistak-
able voice.

What a brilliant animal! He had led me straight to
Claire Mackay. I had met her long ago at the founding
meeting of CANSCAIP but had forgotten she existed
until I started coming to Toronto for the monthly meetings. Then I had noticed her immediately.

I had no idea what she looked like, of course, but
she still stood out. She made the dullest bit of business lively. She got through things in record time without losing her point. I hate dithery, long-winded
speakers. She wrote funny poems. She made me
laugh, and what's more, she made me think.

"He wants you to drop your cookie," I explained now.

"I'm not supposed to feed you," she told him. "Your sign says PLEASE DON'T PET OR FEED ME. I'M WORKING. I can read."

"Yes, but he can't," I said. "He considers you heartless."

Claire, to Zeph's disgust, kept a firm grip on her cookie.

"How's your book coming?" she asked, talking to me and not about my dog. She wasn't being polite. She really wanted to know.

I groaned.

"Oh, it's like that, is it?" said Claire.

She knew. I could tell that she understood exactly how awful it was to have worked on a book for years and still doubt that it would ever be published. This person had never once written a book in an evening.

Someone dragged her away. Zeph sighed so sorrowfully as she took her cookie with her that Audrey promptly fed him two.

On the way home, Jo Ellen and I talked further about writing. She said that writing a picture book was like writing a poem. I privately determined to write one the minute I had a stupendous idea. I would not tell Bob Munsch or Jo Ellen I'd done it until it had been safely accepted, just in case it was far harder than it looked. From now on, I'd be ready to reach out to such a book when it walked past.

But first I had a novel to finish.

During the next year and a bit, I revised *Mama* half a hundred times for Shelley Tanaka. When Clarke Irwin went bankrupt, leaving me free to take my manuscript elsewhere, Shelley and I conferred. The thought of starting again with a new editor made me feel ill.

"Could we submit it to someone with you to edit it?" I asked.

Shelley, now a freelancer, inquired. When she called me back two days later, I could hear the smile in her voice.

"I have offers for *Mama* from five different publishers," she said.

I picked the House I thought was most likely to stay in business. Penguin. The idea of one of my stories actually becoming a Puffin Book clinched it.

David Kilgour, my Penguin editor, and Shelley steered me through yet another revision. I had so many tapes in my bedroom that I was afraid to sneeze lest I cause an avalanche. Finally I went to Shelley's office to do the last once-over.

"Shall I read you what you had and then how I think it should be changed?" she asked, uncertain how to proceed.

"No," I said resolutely, "read it leaving out the bits you've cut. If something important is missing, I'll know. If I don't miss it, it can't have been all that important."

It worked. Here and there I did miss something that mattered to me. When I explained my reasoning to her, Shelley frowned, stared at the script in front of her and came up with a solution. Or I did. What I loved was telling her a better phrase and her never needing to ask where I wanted it to go. She and I worked as one. And I knew the book was going to live when, even after all the years we had both spent fiddling with it, her voice broke as she read the final chapter.

I was at Gilead the day the finished book arrived in Guelph. Mother and her friend Belle made the three-and-a-half hour drive to Muskoka to put it into my hands. As I took it, my eyes filled with tears. I had been so sure that I would never see another published book with my name on the cover. Yet here it was.

Until *Mama's Going to Buy You a Mockingbird* was short-listed for the Ruth Schwartz Award, I had not read one of Claire Mackay's books. Weren't they all about baby "bikers"? But her novel, *The Minerva Program*, was also a contender for the Schwartz prize. Wanting to size up the competition, I asked Mother to read some of it aloud to me one evening.

"We can start it but we mustn't try to finish tonight," Mother warned. "We have a lot to do tomorrow."

At eleven-thirty she glanced guiltily at her watch.

"Go on. Go *on!*"

"I guess we can have one more chapter," she said.

It was almost one o'clock when we finished the book. Mother closed it and said,"I'm sorry, dear, but you can forget about winning the Ruth Schwartz Award. Claire Mackay has it for certain."

It was not a motherly thing to say, but I agreed with her. The Ruth Schwartz jury is made up of children, and children would be entranced by the antics of Minerva and her friends. While I waited for the verdict, I read *One Proud Summer* and discovered that Claire not only could entertain me, she could make me cry.

Mama won the Ruth Schwartz Award, but not unanimously. The jury has lunch with the winning writer. I sat beside a boy who had voted for *The Minerva Program*. "I would have voted for it, too," I told him. He was not surprised.

I had to get to know this woman outside of meetings. People reported to me that she always wore sneakers. Others made jokes about her not owning a skirt. I, too, hate "good" clothes. Wearing pantyhose and dressy shoes was the price you paid for even a small fame — but I considered it an exorbitant price. I was so fond of being comfortable that I had told the family I wished to be buried wearing pyjamas. I could not bear the thought of waiting for Judgement Day stretched out in a coffin flat on my back and eternally dressed up.

When I recognize a kindred spirit, I don't leave things to chance. Blind people can't. The exchanging of smiles, the giving of wordless messages which are second nature for those with vision are not in a sightless person's repertoire. At a meeting, I would not have been able to hear Jenny smile. If I waited for chance to take care of it, Claire and I would continue to chat in that crowded church basement, at conferences, occasionally at a party.

Claire was one of the many guests invited to a party I threw for myself when *Mama* was finally published. But even such a happy occasion was not the time for embarking on a real friendship. As Rosemary had said to me in a long ago letter, ". . . for talking at any depth about personal things, you need to be a twosome."

Claire Mackay had a husband and three sons. She had numerous calls on her time. If I were intrusive, I might end the friendship before it had gotten well started. What friendship needs most is time, talk and shared laughter. I had to be ready to act fast when opportunity knocked.

Opportunity telephoned instead. I got a call inviting me to be a guest on Morningside, a CBC radio program. I was to be on a panel with Newfoundland writer Kevin Major and Newbery-winning author Madeleine L'Engle. I was to be there at eight-thirty in the morning. I had also been invited to a surprise birthday party for Audrey McKim in Toronto that evening.

Perfect. If Mother dropped me off at the CBC studio and Claire met me there, we would have a generous slice of time all to ourselves between the events. If Claire were free . . .

As I waited for her to answer her telephone, all the rebuffs I suffered as a cross-eyed little girl and a dumpy, disabled teenager returned to demolish my self-confidence. I was thankful when she answered on the second ring.

I launched into a confused explanation. I could hear my voice sounding rattled. She made no encouraging noises. I couldn't even hear her breathing. "If you're free," I finished all in a rush, "I could take you out to lunch and then we could spend the afternoon together and then go to Audrey's party. Jo Ellen will drive me home."

She spoke not a word. Why, why had I phoned?

"Well, let me see . . ." said Claire after what seemed like a couple of centuries.

"You don't have to," I stuck in. "But you'll get to meet Madeleine L'Engle . . ."

She laughed at me.

"I can arrange things so that I'm free," she said. "I was just figuring out how, that's all. It sounds great. Where am I to come?"

That afternoon, Claire and I talked about ourselves, our writing, our troubles, our joys. But it was Zephyr who tested this budding friendship and proved it to be all I had hoped.

While Claire got her husband's dinner ready, I took my dog out for a game of ball in the Mackays' large yard. Claire went with me to make sure I was pointed in the right direction.

"Is there anything else you need to know?" she asked.

"No," I said, having no notion there was a large swimming pool off to my left. She returned to domesticity, and I began tossing the balls for Zeph to chase. Everything went well until I, in my ignorance, threw one smack onto the middle of the swimming pool cover. Never having seen such a thing, my Seeing Eye dog raced confidently out onto it.

Riiipppp!

It sounded as though he were tearing up their shrubbery. I called him but, when the unidentifiable sound continued and no Zeph came running back to me, I set out to find him.

He was in the deep end. Most of him was down in the water under the cover. His chin and his two front paws were hooked over the edge of the pool. He looked astonished and very frightened.

I had actually worn a dress and pantyhose to honour Audrey. I went down on my knees and pulled his collar. It slid off over his head. Panicking only slightly, I grabbed the scruff of his neck and hauled him up and out. With a mighty scramble, he arrived at my side. With a mighty shake, he soaked me to the skin.

I forgot all about the ball.

"You fool dog," I scolded, hugging him. I could not get any wetter, and he looked hangdog. Then, not sure how to find my way into the house and loath to go in anyway, dripping, I began to throw more balls for him. It would help us both dry off a bit.

Riiipppp!

Seeing Eye dogs are noted for their intelligence and, up until that moment, I had believed Zeph to be extraordinarily bright. But he had gone right back after the original ball, this time tumbling in at the shallow end.

I rescued him once more, shredding the knees of my pantyhose on the cement.

Then Claire came out. Zephyr and I stood, water running in rivulets off both of us, and looked at her. It was partly sheer shock, I am sure, but she appeared magnificently calm. No gush. No fuss. No apologizing or demanding what on earth I thought I was doing. She actually laughed.

And I knew, for certain, that Zephyr had been right. She was exactly the friend I had been seeking.

❧ 24 ❧

To undertake is to achieve
Be Undertaking blent
With fortitude of obstacle
And toward encouragement.
Emily Dickinson

During that spring, I was preoccupied with raising money for a talking computer named SAM. Months before, on a radio science program, I had heard someone say that audio word processors would soon be available commercially. I had sat bolt upright and stared at the radio. The announcer spoke casually of "voice synthesizers." The program ended. But from then on, I pestered everyone I knew.

"If you ever hear of a talking computer, let me know. If you ever read of an audio word processor, tell me. If anybody ever mentions a computer with a built-in voice, get the name for me."

Jo Ellen was wrapping Christmas presents for her family in Texas, using the Toronto *Star* as padding, when the following headline jumped out at her:

Talking robot that helps blind "see" speaks with a Canadian accent

She called me. Jo Ellen is usually self-controlled even when she is excited, but I knew the minute I heard her voice that she was bursting with good news of some sort.

Half an hour later, I held the story in my hands. It wasn't really about a robot at all. It was just what I had been dreaming of, a "talking computer named SAM." As we pored over the clipping, I tried not to grow too jubilant. But the story claimed that this machine could read back to blind typists the words they had just typed. The initials SAM stood for Synthetic Audio Micro. It had been developed by a blind man named David Kostyshyn. He had started to study dentistry before he lost his vision. Now he had his own company, Syntha Voice Computers, located nearby in Hamilton.

As I waited for morning, when I could phone and find out more, I thought of being able to go back to a keyboard and give up using cassettes. If only it were true!

I reached the young man without trouble. He suggested I come to the office for a demonstration. I made an appointment and then called two friends. Mary Rubio, the friend who had persuaded me to apply for a Canada Council grant when I badly needed one and who had been of enormous help to me in countless other ways, had talked to me excitedly about her first ventures into the computer world. If she was free, she would be able to ask sensible questions. Rhondda Lymburner, another good friend, worked in the local Vocational Rehabilitation Office. She might be interested not only because of me but because of her job. They were both eager to come.

Late at night, after we had been to see and hear this technological miracle, I wrote, with a black marker, in my diary.

> *1 a.m. Dec. 8th (9th really)*
> *I feel I should be writing this in red letters. I went and saw SAM . . . I'll get it somehow . . . I longed to say I would start the course of training on Monday and*

I'd take the machine home with me. But I won't be able to find the money that fast. It seems the answer to all my problems. It'll read out what I've written letter by letter, or the words in sequence. It pauses for commas. You can correct things, find things, edit things, store things etc. etc. It won't be easy for me to learn to operate it . . . but I can . . . My motivation is astronomical . . . Nobody who isn't handicapped can know the wonder of being able to write totally independently.

It took six months to raise the money. I had earned only $15,000 the preceding year, and we had spent most of it on such items as bread, butter, eggs, headache pills and dental bills. I would not have gone to the dentist had I known.

So many people helped. I asked everybody for donations to my SAM fund that Christmas. My friends and relations gave nobly. A group of children in Erin raised enough to pay for my Wordstar program. The Guelph Lions Club bought me a laser printer. Other service clubs and women's groups pitched in.

On May 21st, I went to learn how to use this miracle of a machine. Although I could touch type, I knew nothing about computers. David Kostyshyn had been affable when I was a prospective customer. How would he be as a teacher?

That first morning, he told us to press the Control Key and then, with it held down, to hit each Function Key in turn. When I did, SAM said, "PERSONAL CARD FILE WORDSTAR LOTUS SCANNER DOS COMMANDS." Amazing!

I was feeling self-confident when David was called to the phone. Why not go on experimenting on my own? Obviously, if you held down this Control Key, nothing else worked. I was uncertain about which keys were which around the edges. I had never really mastered the numbers, for instance. I'd just push a few.

David returned to the room in time to hear my SAM cry out in an agitated voice, "Up arrow, error, up arrow, error, error . . .!"

"What have you done?" my teacher yelled at me. "You don't know enough to have gotten an error message!"

My self-confidence collapsed and so did David's faith in me. Zephyr, who had been lying quietly at my feet, sat up and put his head on my lap.

A few sentences from my diary sum up that week.

> *Monday Night May 27*
> *I've waited so long for this day . . . I survived . . .*
> *DAVID ISN'T A PATIENT TEACHER! He barks,*
> *"What did you press that key for?" in such an irritated*
> *voice. I still like him though . . . We worked on that*
> *keyboard for six hours . . . I'm very tired and my head*
> *is aching . . . Yet I can insert, delete, erase, have it read*
> *back . . . I can learn exactly where I am on a page at*
> *a given moment. And I'm growing used to how it*
> *talks. . . .*

> *May 28 10 p.m. Tuesday*
> *I more than survived today. I was prepared for David's*
> *impatience. . . . And I learned SO MUCH. I wrote a*
> *letter to myself. I opened and closed a file. I'm not as*
> *beat and down as I was last night. . .*

> *9:40 p.m. Wednesday*
> *I wrote about the quick brown fox, two paragraphs*
> *worth, and "Now is the time . . . ," one paragraph*
> *worth. We corrected errors and reformed paragraphs.*
> *I think I am doing a bit better . . . Wishful thinking?*

May 30, 1985, Thursday
. . . this morning was really good. I'm starting to be
comfortable with SAM, more comfortable anyway . . .
Only a day and a half to go!

8:30 p.m. Friday
I'm so tired. I feel almost as exhausted as I did on
Monday. But I printed something and set tabs. I did
learn a lot.

It was four o'clock on Friday afternoon. Mother was
waiting to take me home. Several people had gathered
to say goodbye. David faced me, ready for a farewell
exchange. I gripped Zephyr's harness handle and
searched my mind for words to express my gratitude
for the miracle this young man had worked in my life.
I knew that he himself understood. He had been
through the same bitterness and frustration. But I still
had to tell him, thank him. Then I knew how.

"I've never said this to anyone before, David," I said,
keeping my tone light. "I never thought I'd say it to
anyone ever. But I'm glad you lost your sight. If you
hadn't gone blind, you might have turned into a dentist! Then you'd have come up with some fancy drill
instead of working miracles for people like me . . ."

My voice quit. I heard a gasp behind me. But David
understood. He rocked back on his heels and gave a
shout of laughter.

"Call and tell me how things go," he said then. "If
you need help, I'm here."

I had left The Seeing Eye determined that I would
never have to summon aid. I would not make that
mistake this time.

"You'll be hearing from me," I said. "Often!"

I must have phoned a hundred times in the next

few weeks. Never once did he lose his temper. Always, good-humouredly, he solved my problem. Unconsciously, he also injected me with his own humour, optimism and courage.

One of these days, I keep telling myself, I must cross out that bit in my diary about how impatient he is. When it comes to being long-suffering and slow to wrath, he could give Jehovah lessons.

⚥ 25 ⚥

To know her not — Affliction—
To own her for a Friend
A warmth as near as if the Sun
Were shining in your Hand.
Emily Dickinson

"Oh, no!" I cried, snatching the letter away from Mother and pressing my nose to the paper. The words were a blur but, because I had just heard them read aloud, I could make them out.

> *I'm speaking at Ideashop in Toronto next fall. Do you suppose we'll really meet at last?*
>
> > *love,*
> > *Katherine Paterson*

Mother stared at me. "I would have thought you'd be bringing the roof down with shrieks of joy," she said. "What's the matter? Aren't you glad?"

"Of course I'm glad," I said, "I've wanted to meet her for years. I just don't want to be introduced to her at Ideashop. I met Betsy Byars that way and it was awful. You can't say anything that means anything in the middle of a mob, especially when you know everyone within earshot is listening."

My voice trailed away as I thought back to when I had first discovered Katherine Paterson's books. I had a librarian to thank.

"Read this one," she had said, handing me *The Sign of the Chrysanthemum*.

I had recently come home from Japan, so I was curious about what the book had to say. My interest was soon transformed into love for the hero, searching so desperately for the father he had never known. I returned the library copy and bought a hardcover for myself. I got the author's next two books, which were also set in Japan. They allowed me to become an insider where I had, in actuality, always remained a "gaijin" or foreigner. They made me homesick for the tastes and sounds, the landscape and the people I had left in Kanazawa.

I could no longer see well enough to read regular print when *Bridge to Terabithia* was published. I took a paperback copy to Gilead. One hot afternoon, when Mark and Sarah and I were about ready to go swimming, my sister, Pat, picked it up and read the first three or four pages.

"Sit down," she ordered us. "I want to read this book to you."

Mark and Sarah protested.

"We'll go swimming, don't worry," Pat said. "Sit down and listen."

We read all the way to the end and swam after supper. It was a great book. But it made me nervous. Were her Jess and Leslie too much like my Jeremy and Tess? I had just finished the second draft of *Mama's Going to Buy You a Mockingbird*. If only I'd worked harder and gotten it done before this other book came out!

I soon saw how stupid I was being. Katherine Paterson and I could not have all that much in common. Even if we began with the very same plot, we would end up creating entirely different books. Our voices were different. Hers had a Southern accent. She had been born in China, I knew, but she was an American, she had no handicap and she had a husband and four children. I put her new book with the other three and did my best to forget it.

Then Mother read me *The Great Gilly Hopkins* and, although Katherine did not know it yet, she and I became friends. I gave copies of *Gilly* not only to everyone I knew but to several near strangers. When I sent Rosemary one for Christmas, I stopped to make a count. I had personally purchased and distributed over forty copies. It was time I wrote the author a fan letter. After all, I was helping to support her.

Katherine replied. What pleased her most was the knowledge that her Gilly was actually going to Rosemary Sutcliff's house. "I hope she behaves herself," she wrote.

It was not until *Gates of Excellence*, her collection of articles, speeches and reviews, was published in 1983 that I finally learned that Katherine Paterson and I did have a lot in common. As Mother read the autobiographical bits aloud, I kept interrupting to exclaim, "She and I must be exactly the same age!" "She hadn't any friends in grade four either!" "She loves *The Secret Garden* as much as we do!" "She thought Elsie Dinsmore was dumb, too!"

Katherine and I were both missionaries' kids. We had been born and lived our first few years in the Orient. We had both been brought to North America just before World War II, and neither of us had fitted in at school. She, too, had lived in Japan as an adult. She, too, had written a book about foster children, a book about death and only one book in the first person. She was as committed to the Christian church as I was. She had two adopted daughters; I had an adopted niece and nephew.

Her novels also were realistic, and her vision of the world of childhood seemed, to me, close to my own.

Now she was coming to Toronto. We were going to meet. But not at a conference, if I could possibly avoid it.

I wrote inviting Katherine to come a day early, stay overnight at our house and go to Ideashop with me. I promised to invite some other Canadian children's writers to a sukiyaki dinner.

Katherine phoned to accept. When she told me who was calling, I gasped. She heard me and laughed. But all writers are readers first. Even when you yourself have become a writer and have other authors as friends, there is still powerful magic in speaking with the person who created Galadriel Hopkins and Maime Trotter.

"I'd love to come," said Katherine Paterson.

Claire took me to the airport. She was as eager to meet Katherine as I was. Janet Lunn and Barbara Greenwood joined us. We had a glorious time. There was never an instant of awkward silence. There was hardly a silence at all.

The week before, I had shown a woman my computer. She had looked from my technological miracle to my Wonder Dog and gushed, "How lovely! All your problems are solved, aren't they?"

Katherine was fascinated by SAM. She did not think my problems were all solved, however.

"Even with its help, I don't know how you do it," she said. "It's hard enough, Lord knows, when you can see perfectly well."

We spent what time we could together throughout the conference. Jo Ellen and I drove her to the airport. The visit I had been looking forward to for months was, all at once, only a jumble of blurred memories. I felt bereaved. I acted grouchy.

Then Katherine wrote.

> *You couldn't know how much I've been living with you since I left Toronto. I had to fly to Vermont two weeks ago and took* From Anna *with me, since it was a book of yours I hadn't read yet, and sat there boo-hooing on the airplane . . . I felt badly not to have read it before, somehow it was perfect to read it after having met you.*

Way to go, Anna.

The letter ended with an invitation to visit her in Norfolk, Virginia. I went that May. We talked and talked — and talked some more. I told her I'd been asked to go to England with three other Canadian writers, on an exchange visit with some British writers who would tour Canada in the fall. We were to go to Britain for a week in November.

"The thing is," I said, "I want to stay longer and visit Rosemary. And I'll have to leave Zephyr behind because of their quarantine laws. You wouldn't by any chance be interested in coming along as my guide person, would you?"

I wasn't joking. With Zephyr to pilot me, I was able to find chairs, locate curbs, follow other people, return to the right hotel room and feel in command of most situations. Without him or a stand-in, I was lost.

I also was certain Katherine and I would have a lovely time travelling together. But that went without saying.

"I'd introduce you to Rosemary," I said, certain that even with such a bribe, Katherine would be unable to accept.

She actually checked. She couldn't make it on those

dates. Then our tour was postponed until February, and she decided to come. After all, what other chance would she have to visit England as a Seeing Eye dog?

Before we left, I wrote the first eight chapters of an autobiographical book called *Little by Little*. It started out as an account of my adventures with Zephyr, his training and his reformation, but David Kilgour asked me to "expand it a bit."

"I've heard you tell some great stories about your childhood," he said. "Just work in a couple of those."

I hesitated.

"Once I get started on my childhood, David," I said, "you might end up with an entirely different book."

David is a good editor. "Fine. Go ahead," he said.

He called to see how I was progressing. "I've done what you asked me to," I said. "I've expanded the manuscript. I've finished eight chapters."

"How old are you at the end of Chapter Eight?"

"Seven," I said.

I hated leaving Zephyr behind when I went to England. I felt myself that the British should make an exception when it came to guide dogs. Guide dog owners, after all, would never fail to safeguard the health of their dogs or let them run free in a strange country.

Yet, much as I admired Zeph's many skills, I soon realized that Katherine told better stories. I also appreciated not having to take her out at regular intervals. And I didn't have to keep apologizing for the hairs she shed or for her imploring gaze being fixed upon the tasty morsel in someone's hand. She was good at guiding, too. She had watched Zephyr work and had decided that her best course would be to use his methods.

Over and over during those two weeks, the people

we were with were sure she was neglecting me. What they failed to observe was that Katherine, like Zephyr, simply paused to warn me of down steps or curbs. Since I was holding her elbow, she was, again like Zephyr, a step ahead of me. When she stepped up, I always knew in plenty of time to do likewise. If an obstruction loomed overhead or underfoot, she steered me around it by drawing her elbow in closer to her body and moving sideways, leaving space enough for both of us to be safe. Zephyr, after all, manages these feats without speaking a word, and I am accustomed to reading his body language.

"It's marvellous," others kept saying in puzzled tones, "how you seem to read each other's minds . . ."

I had chosen well. She made a topnotch dog.

My companions phoned home as soon as we arrived to report on the journey and check on their families. I did not. I knew that Zephyr was either pining for me, which would break my heart, or not pining at all, which would be almost as hard to bear. I kept thinking about the wounded way he had stared at me when I started out the door with my suitcase. I longed to know what had happened next. I didn't call to ask.

Once we were settled in our hotel, Katherine and I decided to go to Evensong before dinner. We asked at the desk whether there would be a service that night. They couldn't say. We went anyway. We arrived at the churchyard gate at about 5:20. There was no activity, but there was a light shining above the door. We hesitated. Our taxi driver sighed loudly. Indecision was costing money.

"We can get another cab if we need one," I murmured.

Katherine paid him and he drove off. The sky darkened perceptibly as he disappeared. The two of us ventured through the open gate and up the walk, although there was as yet no sign of even a token congregation. We tried the door. It was locked fast. We prowled around for awhile, hoping other worshipers would materialize. Nobody came. It was cold and getting dark when Katherine finally spotted an elderly man shambling towards the church.

"Wait here," she said. "I'll ask if there's a service."

I waited. Then she bolted back and clutched my arm.

"Is he . . .?" I began.

"No, he isn't," she hissed. "Come on. I'll tell you later."

We hustled down the road till we were out of sight of the church.

"What did he say?" I demanded then.

"Nothing. Once I got close, I saw he was not opening the church; he was relieving himself against the church wall. I didn't stay to chat."

We were standing there shaking with suppressed laughter, both at her discomfiture and at our present predicament, when the rain began. We had no idea where our hotel was. Our taxi was long gone. The road was devoid of cars. It was growing dark fast. And the gentle drizzle was icy and growing heavier by the minute.

"Zephyr would never have gotten you lost on the very first night," mourned my friend.

That was probably true, but I would not have made the exchange if I could. I told her so. She turned up her coat collar and muttered something I could not quite hear. It sounded like something no Presbyterian minister's wife should say.

We set out down the wet street in search of a cab. Apparently the taxi business had closed up for the night. We passed dark, silent houses set far back from the road, and anonymous businesses and warehouses all shut. We were decidedly wet when we at last spotted some sort of shop with a lighted window. I stayed in the dry doorway while Katherine plunged in. I could hear the people inside laughing at the lost foreigners. But they called a cab for us. "It'll pull up at the corner, ducks," they said. If only we were ducks, I thought, shivering in my wet coat.

We arrived back at the hotel at eight o'clock, soaked through, tired out and very hungry. As we dressed in dry clothes and, looking only slightly bedraggled, sat down to an excellent dinner, I smiled at Katherine.

"Did I ever tell you about the time Zephyr fell into the Mackays' swimming pool?" I asked.

The next afternoon the whole Canadian contingent — authors Monica Hughes, Camilla Gryski and Kathy Stinson plus Kathy Lowinger, the Director of the Children's Book Centre — went to tea at Rosemary Sutcliff's. I felt guilty landing in on her with such a crowd, but she made everyone feel so at home that Monica even managed not to die of embarrassment when she upset the cream pitcher.

Barnaby and Sebastian, Rosemary's valiant and vociferous chihuahuas, made me miss Zephyr. Whatever the size or conformation, a dog is a dog. Sebastian, famous for his ability to sense people's distress, hopped lightly up on my lap and, curling into a neat circle, lay there for a few solacing moments. Barney stuck to Rosemary, in case we turned out to be dangerous.

It took me awhile to realize why it mattered so much to me that I was in England as a writer rather than as a tourist. While I listened to British boys and girls laughing at Katherine's dramatic reading of a scene in my book

Different Dragons, I remembered myself at their age believing that all the good stories happened in London or Yorkshire or the Lake District. Yet these youngsters were clearly enjoying hearing about Ben diving under his bed during a thunderstorm — only to discover that the big dog he dreads is under there with him. Ben did not mean to them what Mary Lennox had meant to me but, nevertheless, Ben Tucker who lived in Ontario had won a place in their hearts.

Finding a copy of *Mama's Going to Buy You a Mockingbird* sitting on a shelf at Foyle's Bookstore, along with novels by Clive King and E. Nesbit and Jill Paton Walsh and C. S. Lewis, gave me the same shiver of delight. What was so lovely was that the bookstore people had not known we were coming. Jeremy and Tess had made it there all on their own. And Jess and Leslie from *Bridge to Terabithia* were on the next shelf down. Katherine and I left with armloads of books. It was the least we could do.

Halfway through our second week, the suspense proved too much, and I called home. The moment Mother said, "Dr Little speaking," I blurted, "It's me. How's Zephyr?"

"His sorrow has not overwhelmed his appetite," my mother said.

She went on to tell me that my dog had gone to bed right after I had left and had stayed there alone in my room waiting for my return. He had not relaxed his vigil until she called him for breakfast the next morning.

"Ever since, he's acted normally," she said, "but I don't think you need to worry about his not being glad to see you when you come home. We'll both be pleased, as a matter of fact."

The most memorable hour of the trip came near its

end. We were sauntering down a village street with John Rowe Townsend and Jill Paton Walsh. They paused by a garden gate and quietly conferred. Katherine and I heard the words, "Mrs Boston," but we knew it couldn't be *the* Mrs Boston. We didn't look at each other.

"If only she were in the garden . . ." Jill began.

As if on cue, out from behind some shrubbery came a very old lady who hailed them with the words, "I was hoping to see you two."

"We were hoping to see you as well," Jill said. "We have two writer friends visiting us from America and Canada, and we wanted them to meet you and to see your house."

Under her breath, she muttered to us, "It's Lucy Boston. She's ninety-five and we didn't want to disturb her. But we knew . . ."

Then she introduced us. Katherine and I, overawed and as speechless as either of us is capable of being, went through the garden gate and stared around us in wonder. We had both read and loved the Green Knowe books. We felt privileged to be in this fabled garden. And, of course, even more honoured to meet this remarkable woman and be shown the house where we, along with Tolly and Ping, had gone to stay with old Mrs Oldknow.

We strolled around, beholding with wide eyes the moat and the sculptured yew trees. It was like walking in a dream, except that Mrs Boston was entirely real. Jill told us that her house was perhaps the oldest constantly lived-in house in Britain. She herself wanted to believe there were Anglo-Saxon touches, but Mrs Boston would not allow this.

"Norman," she stated, as though she'd watched it being built.

Standing there, staring at an arrow slit, I realized that Katherine and I were being ridiculous when we called our houses, built over one hundred years ago, "old." They were mere babies. Mrs Boston's house had been more than twice that age before Columbus sailed the ocean blue.

She took us in and, before she offered us a glass of sherry, led us through the rooms. Because she had written, in *The Chimneys of Green Knowe*, the story of the blind girl, Susan, she was particularly eager to have me, too, go away with a clear impression of her home. She took my hands and placed them so that I could feel the incredible thickness of the walls, the immensity of the stone fireplace and the worn stone face carved above it. The cold of the stone floors penetrated the soles of my shoes, and I wondered how those Normans had stood the winters.

"I shan't climb up," Mrs Boston said then to Katherine and me, "but if you go up those stairs, you can see the children's room."

We climbed, our breathing quickening with excitement, and Katherine opened the door. There was no rope across it, no guide's voice relentlessly explaining everything. We walked in, stepping softly. The rocking horse stood there. A small sword hung from a hook. There was the empty birdcage. Two narrow beds covered with patchwork quilts waited side by side for the children — Linnet and Toby, Tolly and Ping and Susan.

I put out my hand and touched the old horse. He rocked gently. I could have sworn I heard children's laughter. We ourselves did not speak above a whisper. You don't when you are under a spell.

What gave that hour its magic was not simply the

antiquity of the house or the fame of its mistress. It lay in the fact that we had been there before in our imaginations.

The day before Katherine and I left for North America, we went down to Sussex again to visit Rosemary on our own. In the train we began talking of the burden and bother and bliss of writing novels. I knew that Katherine would not discuss a book she had not yet finished. She was not alone in this. Although I am happy to discuss my current work with whoever sounds interested, I know it is risky. Books that are talked about too much are in danger of never getting written. Friends may give you advice which, well meant though it may be, can deflect you from your own vision. All the same, I was consumed with curiosity about what she was working on. She seemed in such a good mood. We'd just spent a joyous two weeks together. It couldn't hurt to try.

"Can I ask you a question about your book?" I ventured.

It was like watching Jekyll turn to Hyde. Blind as I was, I saw her stiffen and felt the temperature drop to below zero.

"You know I don't talk about my books while I'm writing them," she snarled.

"Okay, okay. Never mind. Forget it."

"What do you want to know?" There was no warmth in the growled words. I had meant to ask what the story was about, but I hurriedly switched to something nobody in her right mind could resent.

"Is it about a boy or a girl?" I said humbly.

"Boy." She let a few seconds pass before she added, "But there's a girl in it, too."

I sat very still and kept quiet. Finally she added one more grudging snippet. "It's what I always write about. You know. Boy with no father searches for father and finds someone else is his real father."

We did not mention the subject again.

Katherine's husband, John, met her in Montreal while I flew on to Toronto. After she said goodbye, I leaned my head back and closed my eyes. Our trip was over and I was so tired. Then I remembered Zephyr and smiled.

"He's in the car," Mother said when she met me. "He's so strong that I didn't dare bring him into the airport."

I looked at my small parent. "I'm glad," I told her.

As we approached the car, I longed to be able to see for myself what was happening. Mother read my mind.

"He hasn't seen us . . . oh, he's looking this way," she told me. "He's standing up. Look at that tail go! He's one happy dog!"

I pulled open the rear door. He shot out like a cannonball. He romped around me, knowing he must not jump but, finally, unable to keep his ecstatic paws on the ground. I bent to hug him and had my face thoroughly washed by an enormous tongue.

"I'm pleased to see you, too," I said. "Yes, I know. It's me. Yes. Good boy. Yes. I came home. Okay. Settle down. *Down!*"

Except for the tail, he obeyed at once. After all, he was a Seeing Eye dog. His mistress had returned to him. It was time to get back to work.

Claire and I were in the Patersons' kitchen in Vermont when the subject of Katherine's book next came up. I knew it was finished, because she had told me over the phone about the trouble they were having choosing a title. She had not told me the plot, but I had learned my lesson. Like everyone else close to Katherine, including her immediate family, I waited for whatever scraps she let fall. I thought I had warned Claire to avoid asking questions but, if I had, she had not believed I meant it.

"What's your new book about?" she inquired, innocently taking her life in her hands.

I held my breath. But Katherine answered civilly. "I can tell you the plot," she said, "but there's more to it than that."

"Of course," I murmured, nudging Claire not to push her luck. Claire got the message and settled for merely looking interested. John grinned at us sympathetically. Katherine laughed but did not break down and explain herself. I brought up the title debate.

"We've settled on *Park's Quest*," she volunteered. Well, that was better than nothing, I thought.

I had brought her a set of bound galleys of *Little by Little*. She read it the following afternoon. I waited in my bedroom across the hall, every nerve taut. Claire came in and kept me company. We heard sounds issuing from behind Katherine's door.

"She's either laughing or crying," Claire said. "I'm not sure which."

I was too tense to respond. Katherine emerged. She was in tears. She hugged me and I felt as though I'd won the Nobel Prize.

We were at a Fellowship Dinner at the Patersons' church the next day, when Katherine looked at Claire and said in a highly self-conscious voice, "Claire, since you were a medical social worker, I'd be grateful . . . you'd be doing me a real favour . . . if you'd read my

Claire, Katherine and I.

manuscript and tell me if I have the part about the grandfather's stroke right. Seriously, it would help me out if . . ."

Claire was dumbfounded. I was outraged.

"You *wouldn't*," I half yelled. "You couldn't be going to let Claire read your book when I can't!"

Katherine looked at me. I was about to throw a full-scale tantrum right there in the church basement. She laughed.

"All right, little girl," she mocked. "If you're going to make a scene, I'll read it aloud to both of you. Will that do?"

I was jubilant. We were actually going to hear the book I'd wondered about for so long. And Katherine herself was going to read it. I had heard her read aloud. I could hardly wait.

We were settled on the couch, listening, before I began to worry. What if we didn't like the book? Well, we would like it, but what if we didn't love it? She'd know. One look at us and she'd know.

I prayed it would be wonderful and knew that Claire was praying right along with me.

Parkington Waddell Broughton the Fifth was an endearing hero. I liked him from the beginning. And Thanh captured my heart in much the same way that Gilly Hopkins had. The story began well. It made me laugh. It moved me. But could it go on growing in power all the way to the end? What if it came apart halfway?

I had ostentatiously wiped away a tear or two, when John came to the door and offered to read the second half to save Katherine's voice. She handed the book over. I hoped he read as well as she did. I also hoped I'd cry a little more.

John read one chapter and, all at once, the Patersons' living room was awash. Katherine watched us become overwhelmed by pity and grief and she drew a long, relieved breath. If *Park's Quest* could make three adults weep like this, it must be all right. Claire and I weren't thinking about her any longer. We were inside the book, being torn apart and healed. John was reading the last page. John was coming to the final sentence.

Then, reaching those singing words, John Paterson became utterly unintelligible.

We laughed at him while we gulped and sniffed. He didn't mind. No wonder Katherine talked about him so lovingly.

After we'd mopped our wet faces, and John and Katherine had left the room, Claire and I tiptoed to where the manuscript was lying. Keeping one eye on the door, she whispered the bit we had missed. No wonder it did John in.

Zephyr had had enough. He stretched, gave a distinctly bored yawn and got to his feet.

"I'll go out with you. I need some air," Claire said.

When we were at a safe distance, I asked her if she had been as nervous as I.

"Of course," she said.

We walked along in silence for a moment. It was twilight. The snow that had fallen all afternoon had stopped.

Claire spoke into the silence, her voice filled with wonder. "She's won two National Book Awards and two Newberys and I swear she was afraid we wouldn't like it. She was scared! Katherine Paterson was scared."

"I know," I said. "But this book is brand new. You know how you feel at that stage. Half proud, half terrified."

"But she's Katherine Paterson," Claire repeated. "What does it matter to her what we think about it? Who are we?"

I knew what she meant. But I knew the answer, too.

"We're her readers," I said, "and the minute she stops being afraid that her best isn't good enough, she'll stop being Katherine Paterson."

I pulled Zephyr out of a clump of tall grass.

"Come on," I said. "It's time we went back and told her our favourite bits. It's all very well to be assured your book is wonderful, but you hunger for specificity."

We started back. As we reached the bottom of the front steps, Claire said softly, "It's comforting, isn't it, to know that she's just like the rest of us."

"Yes," I said. "But don't ask her what she's starting on next, not if you want to stay friends."

"Are you serious?"

"Try it and see," I said and led the way inside.

⚓ 26 ⚓

He ate and drank the precious Words—
His Spirit grew robust—
He knew no more that he was poor,
Nor that his frame was Dust—

He danced along the dingy Days
And this Bequest of Wings
Was but a Book — What Liberty
A loosened spirit brings—
                    Emily Dickinson

I leafed through my mail and let out a groan.

"Fan letters?" Mother asked sympathetically.

"Two thin ones and *four* class sets! Oh, how I hate . . ."

". . . being a Class Project," she finished for me. "But maybe some of these children chose on their own to thank you for writing their favourite book."

"Maybe." But, looking at the four fat brown envelopes filled with sheets and sheets of faint pencilled writing, I doubted it.

"Do you want me to read them to you now?"

"I don't *want* you to read them to me ever," I told her.

Yet we went through them after supper. I did not have time to answer over fifty letters, but I had to check that no child needed a fast answer. No one did, although everyone wanted me to reply. Nobody had put in a self-addressed envelope or postage.

I have to do a project and I chose you . . .

My class has to write to a live Canadian and I got you . . .

My class read From Anna. *At the end of every chapter we had to do a stencil.*

"That's *awful!*" I wailed. "I didn't write the book for that."

"Listen to this one!" My mother was also outraged.

I am in a Gifted Program and I have to do research on a writer. Please answer the following questions.

"Well, at least she said please," I muttered.

"But there are twelve questions here," Mother said. "Getting you to tell her all the answers — what sort of research is that? She's not gifted; she's lazy."

The next three letters were exact duplicates of hers. The only difference was in the signatures. They all had chosen to "do research" by sending me a list of questions to answer. None mentioned ever having read one of my books.

Answering such letters took hours of my time, even if I were as rude as I yearned to be, and every three letters I sent cost me over a dollar in postage. With few exceptions, teachers earned far more than writers. They'd hit the roof if they had to spend hundreds of dollars on stamps for such letters. If teachers couldn't work, a supply was hired by their school board. When writers couldn't work because they were helping out with billions of class projects, nobody did our real job for us. But if I were to say all of this in my letter back, I would be the one in trouble. I knew. I had tried it twice.

Then Mother laughed. "Here's one that's different," she said.

> *Dear Miss Little,*
> *My class had to read your book* From Anna *for a novel study. I hated it. Why didn't you put some humour in? Why didn't you make it into a mystery? I asked to do a different book but she would not let me. Our workbook says, ''Would you like to read another book about this family?'' My answer is ''No way!!!''*
>
> *Yours truly,*
> *Jack Black*
>
> *P.S. Write back please and send me your autograph. Send two. My friend wants one.*

"Of all the nerve!" I sputtered, but I was laughing, too. It was refreshing to get a letter that wasn't prefabricated by the teacher. I had had so many that gave me the child's name, age, birthday, hair and eye colour, names of family members and pets, hobbies, favourite part of the book they'd studied and ended up asking seven questions and demanding that I write back *soon*.

"Well, you needn't answer these now," my mother said, bundling them into the overflowing To Be Answered box. "We can do them after the tour. You'll be inspired by meeting your readers face to face."

I snorted. The week-long Book Festival tours organized annually by the Children's Book Centre were more exhausting than inspiring. Yet I was pleased to be going. And Zephyr, always a sucker for an audience, positively loved Book Festival.

Four evenings later I was on my way to a small mining town in western Canada. My driver was concentrating on the road. We were breaking the speed limit, and I was glad because we were going to be very late as it was. My itinerary read, "6:00 p.m. Dinner at home of Molly Cameron, fifth grade teacher." My talking watch said, "It is 7:09 p.m." I hoped Miss Cameron had not counted on us being punctual.

As we pulled up in front of my hotel, my driver said, "There's Wendy Legatt, the library consultant. She'll be driving you around while you're here."

He swung out of the van and began explaining that we had had car trouble en route. Wendy only half listened.

"Let's unload your stuff," she said, "and then, if you don't mind, let's go. I told Molly we'd be there an hour ago."

I dumped my suitcase on the bed and hurried back to her. I hated being late. Especially when someone had a meal waiting.

"Where will Zephyr ride?" Wendy asked as we ran to her car.

"On the floor in the front. He'll sit between my feet."

She eyed his bulk doubtfully. "My car's small," she began.

"It doesn't matter," I told her. "He folds up. You'll see."

As usual, he and I both fitted neatly into the space provided. We sped down a few streets and parked before a private home. We met our hostess, apologized at length and sat down to a marvellous dinner.

Molly Cameron did not say much. She simply plied us with one mouth-watering dish after another. When, replete, we returned to the living room, Wendy and I got onto the subject of bibliotherapy. I disapproved of it. That is, I didn't think you could or should pre-scribe a book to solve a child's problems. I did believe, though, that all book lovers found healing in much that they read. I knew I had in *Outcast* and *Watership Down* and so many more. They had been the morning stars in the "evening of the brain."

Molly Cameron sat listening to the two of us holding forth.

When I paused to draw breath, she said quietly, "I don't know about that. All I do know is that you have worked a miracle in my classroom."

I stared at her.

"I did?" I said weakly.

"Yes," she said. "And I'm really glad you are here so that I can tell you about it in person."

Not sure what to expect, I settled myself to listen.

"Simon joined my class this past September," she said, "and I admit I wasn't looking forward to having him. Ever since his dad moved here three years ago, no teacher has been able to get through to this boy."

"I moved here about the same time," Wendy said, "and I've been hearing about Simon ever since I began visiting the school. He's not your usual trouble-maker. I mean, he's not always throwing his weight around or picking fights."

"I have sometimes wished he would," Molly took up the story. "I could have handled that. No, Simon just sits there and doesn't respond to anything or anybody. When you ask him a direct question, he just shrugs or mutters, 'I don't know.' He never puts up his hand, never volunteers. When he's supposed to bring his French book, he forgets — every time. For two years teachers have been trying to get him to write. He looks at you and the minute you go on to somebody else, he goes right back to printing. He acts as though he's only half there. On his good days, that is."

"Does he have brothers and sisters?" I asked.

"A couple of stepbrothers who've already left home. He's the child of a second marriage, and it hasn't worked out. He lives with his dad, who's no role model, if you know what I mean."

I nodded.

"Well, I was at my wit's end about what to do with him when Wendy came to tell me that our town was having its first author visit," Molly said.

"I said Jean Little was coming," Wendy went on, "and confess, Molly, that you had never heard of her or her books."

"You didn't have to tell her that," the teacher protested.

"Don't worry," I reassured her. "The world is full of people who have never heard of me."

"Well, I've certainly heard of you now," Molly said, not giving Wendy a chance to make it worse. "She put a copy of *From Anna* into my hands and said sixteen kids from my class would get to hear you and wouldn't it mean more if I read them this book? So I started. And, after a couple of days, I saw that Simon was listening!"

The astonishment she had felt still sounded in her voice, even though this had all happened several weeks before.

"I always read the class a book," she said. "But I wasn't sure how this bunch would react. My class last year loved *Charlotte's Web*, but this year's class is rowdier, harder to handle. From the first day, I was grateful to you for giving me a quiet half hour. But I never dreamed that Simon would be interested in the book."

I understood completely. Who would guess that a story about a nine-year-old German immigrant child with poor eyesight and several chips on her shoulder would claim the attention of such a class, let alone win over this withdrawn, "spaced out" ten-year-old boy? I thought of poor Jack Black and grinned.

"You must realize that never before had I seen him listen," Molly told me earnestly. "Oh, now and then he'd seem to be for a second or two. But he'd always go back to staring at nothing. This time I kept glancing over every so often without letting him see I'd noticed. And he went on listening day after day."

They finished the second-last chapter on a Thursday afternoon. As Molly closed the book, she told the children that there was only one chapter left and that they would finish the book the next day. A few minutes later, as she was bending over some work on her desk, she heard a voice say, "Miss."

She looked up. Simon was standing there, his eyes on her face.

"Yes, Simon," she said, trying not to show her surprise.

"Miss," he repeated huskily, "what are you going to do with the book when we've finished it?"

Speaking matter-of-factly, she said, "Well, I suppose I'll put a card in the back and then anyone who wants to can borrow it."

"Can I have it?" Simon asked.

"Certainly," his teacher said, still struggling to hide her astonishment. "You are the first one to ask, so you can be the first one to take it out."

"I stared after him as he walked out the door," she told me. "I couldn't believe it. But the next day, when we finished the story, he was waiting to take it from me. I warned him that he'd have to bring it back on Monday and, to be honest, I wondered if I'd ever see it again.

But on Monday morning, although he had not done any of his homework, he had *From Anna* in his hand. And he carried it around with him all day long."

She had the class write book reviews of the story for me.

"Write down what you liked best about the book," she instructed.

"If we didn't like something, should we put that in?" one of the other boys asked.

"It wasn't that he didn't like it . . ." Molly began to reassure me.

"I know. It's a good question," I said. "What did you answer?"

"Before I had a chance to reply, Simon whirled around in his seat and glared at the other child. 'Not like it!' he cried. 'I *love* that book.'

"The whole class stared at him in amazement. None of us had ever heard him speak passionately about anything before that moment. Nothing more was said about not liking the book. They all got to work on their reviews."

Some wrote half a page. Most wrote a page or two. Simon wrote three-and-a-half pages. His review mentioned every moment of tenderness between Anna and her father in the early chapters. "Then Papa gave Anna a big hug . . ." it read. And a line or two later, "Then Papa gave Anna's hand a warm squeeze."

He also mentioned Miss Williams, Anna's loving teacher.

"The teacher liked Anna a lot," his review read. "Miss Williams saw that Anna was smart."

They wrote rough drafts and then copied them out "nicely" to give to me. As Miss Cameron passed Simon's desk, he looked up at her, his eyes gleaming.

"I'm writing this, Miss," he told her. "I'm not print-ing. I'm writing this for Miss Little."

But only sixteen children could go to the library to hear me. Who would get to go? Simon was worried. So were the rest. How was Miss Cameron going to choose?

The resource teacher, who worked with Simon among others, visited the school that day.

"Simon," she said, "what would you like as a reward for getting ten of these arithmetic questions right?"

"All I want," he said, "is to go to see Jean Little."

The resource teacher went to Molly Cameron.

"Is there any way we can arrange for Simon to be one of the children who gets to meet Jean Little?" she asked.

Molly Cameron smiled, telling me about this.

"I said, 'Simon could do murder and he'd still get to go.'"

But she had to choose the others. Finally she got each of the children to write down why he or she wanted to be among the lucky ones picked to attend the author visit. When they had all done so, each one read his or her reason onto a tape which would be presented to me along with the book reviews.

"I want to go because I never saw an otter," Lucy said.

"I think I should be picked because I have never met a talented person," said Donald.

"I want to see the dog," Joshua said. "He is a See-ing Eye dog. They are extremely clever and excellent. They keep the person from getting hit by cars and trucks. They are specially trained . . ."

Then came Simon's voice, hoarse with feeling.

"I want to go to see Jean Little because I love her books very much," he said. "It would be the thrill of a lifetime . . . I am *begging* you . . . *please* . . . let me go."

As Miss Cameron told me this, I could feel my throat tightening. I blinked away tears.

"Well," I said, "even if it comes to nothing, it is wonderful that he has had such a joyous experience with one book . . ."

Miss Cameron interrupted me.

"But it hasn't come to nothing," she told me emphatically. "When we finished *Listen for the Singing*, the same thing happened. And he's writing now and talking. He's come to life, in a way. He is a changed boy. I told you, you worked a miracle in my classroom."

That night I lay awake in my hotel room thinking about Simon. The next morning I would meet him, Miss Cameron had told me, because he had been picked to give me the tape they had made. She herself would not be there. She had chosen to stay behind with the twelve unlucky ones.

"After all," she said, "I got to spend this evening with you."

I thought about that. And suddenly the whole story started making more sense.

Although I knew that a book could mean a great deal to a child, no boy like Simon is so transformed simply by hearing one novel read aloud. In my book, Anna, who is, like Simon, an unresponsive and difficult child, gets a teacher who shows her that she matters. And, with the encouragement of Miss Williams, Anna slowly comes out of her shell and dares to smile and make friends.

Miss Cameron, I decided, was the Miss Williams in Simon's life. And when he heard about Anna — prickly, closed in, a failure loved only by her father —

actually changing into a different Anna, he looked at Miss Cameron and decided to risk it himself.

Oh, I don't believe he made this decision consciously. All the same, his realization that in Molly Cameron he had his own Miss Williams must have been at the heart of the miracle.

As Zephyr guided me straight to the chair at the front of the packed hall the next morning, the children gasped. My dog had upstaged me again. I did not mind. He was a great help when it came to keeping the attention of kids indifferent or even hostile to books.

"Down, boy," I said.

Zephyr looked at my audience and waited for them to laugh before he sank slowly to a prone position. As his body hit the floor, he gave a groan of protest. The children were convulsed with mirth. I could not help laughing myself. He knew exactly how to get the attention he loved and still coax a "Good boy" out of me.

I told them stories about Zephyr first and then went on to tell them about myself as a little girl who loved to write. I had to make it entertaining. The children in the front row were only in grade one. But I was holding my own. Not one of them had ripped apart the Velcro fastenings on his shoes.

I asked if anyone had a question.

"Can you see us?"

"Not really." I said. "I can see the lights on the windows. I can see blurred shapes but I wouldn't know you were children. You might be monkeys."

"Why don't you write picture books?" a small voice sitting in the front piped up.

I smiled in the voice's direction. "I've started to do that very thing," I said. "My niece, Maggie, and I have just written one together. It's called *Once Upon a*

Golden Apple. Phoebe Gilman is going to draw the pictures."

"Where did you get the idea?" an older child asked.

"From a two-year-old girl named Susanna and her big brother, Jonathan," I told them. "Their parents overheard them pretending to read and saying, 'Once upon a banana . . .' 'No,no,no.' 'Once upon a bicycle . . .' 'No,no,no.' 'Once upon a tree . . .' 'No,no,no.' 'Once upon a time . . .' '*Yes!*' Maggie and I decided to write a whole book that way. Do you want to hear how it goes?"

"Yes," they chorused. They listened almost in silence until I got to the page about Princess Briar Rose:

> *She kissed a cow with a crumpled horn. No.*
> *She kissed a reluctant dragon. No,no,no.*
> *She kissed Humpty Dumpty. No,no,no,no,no.*
> *She kissed a frog. Yes!*

Their burst of spontaneous laughter was music to my ears. I should have done a book for these little ones long ago. No wonder Jo Ellen Bogart and Bob Munsch were so pleased by the response they got.

Was Simon laughing?

"How long did it take you to write it?" asked another child.

"We wrote the first version in one evening," I admitted. "But then we kept changing it. We began it over a year ago, and we just sent in a new version last week."

Suddenly Zephyr, who had gone solidly to sleep, began to snore. "Oh," gasped my audience in shocked delight. I woke Zeph up and scolded him for not listening. The moment I let go of his head, he went right back to sleep.

"How do you feed your dog?" inquired a solemn third grader.

"Well," I said, keeping my voice as solemn as hers, "I take his dish and I go to the dog food bag and scoop out some food and put it into the dish. Then I go to the tap and run a little warm water on it. Then I put it down for him. How do you feed your dog?"

She giggled. "I do the same thing."

It was fun making them rethink what a blind person could do, but all the time I talked, I was waiting for the moment when Simon would present the cassette. Yet when the time came, he did not appear. A girl gave it to me instead. I later learned that Simon had got cold feet at the last moment and thrust it into her hand. I longed to ask about him, but it would have been a breach of confidence.

Quite a story. It made the whole tour worthwhile. It made all the tours in the future mean more. It made stars come out within.

I went home and listened to the tape. I heard twenty-eight ten-year-old children saying why they longed to be chosen to go to see the lady who had written *From Anna*. And I had no idea which twelve had had to stay behind.

I wrote them a letter, called each child by name and answering questions they said they wanted to ask me.

I thought about Simon responding to Anna's story with such fierce delight, and I also sent the class a copy of *The Secret Garden*. Ever since it had first been read aloud to me when I was seven, it had remained the most magical book I knew.

I wrote five pages single-spaced, and I enclosed a picture of Zephyr in case Joshua had been one of the twelve left behind.

It was not like answering the class sets of demanding letters that thud through my mail box daily. The children in Miss Cameron's class had not asked me for anything. They had given to me instead by loving my Anna so much. They had asked only that I keep writing stories. They had even said thank you.

If only every Simon had a Miss Cameron, I thought, because the miracle had happened not as a result of the author visit but before I had even arrived. It had been Anna . . .

Then I remembered Jack Black. Instead of exiting Word Perfect, I turned back to my computer and opened a new file.

> *Dear Jack Black,*
> *I don't blame you for not wanting to read* From Anna.
> *I'm sorry I didn't put more humour in for you. I like mysteries, too, but I don't think I'd be good at writing them. I love Anna myself but I don't see why you should have to. Tell your teacher, from me, that I think you should get to choose. I'll bet you'd like* The Minerva Program *by Claire Mackay. It is funny and mysterious both. Keep reading a Little, Jack. The best place for your nose is inside a book.*
>
> > *Sincerely,*
> > *Jean Little*
>
> *P.S. Have you read* The Great Gilly Hopkins *by Katherine Paterson? It is very funny — and a little mysterious. I love it. Let me know what you think.*
>
> > *J.L.*

EPILOGUE

In 1970 I wrote a poem about Emily Dickinson. I wrote it immediately after buying and reading the variorum editions of her letters and poems published by The Belknap Press. My poem was only six verses long then but, over the years, I have revised and added to it. Despite its length, I feel it belongs in this book.

How singular was Emily,
Her startled being full
Of cryptic visions her world found
Unintelligible.

Held captive by her genius
Nor seeking to break free
From walls which kept inviolate
Her inner liberty;

Yet longing to communicate,
Lonely enough to try.
Did she not know her messages;
Forgot to tell them why?

Baffled children scanned her notes.
Neighbours pondered on
Lines which hid their meaning in
Her private lexicon.

She set the puzzles tenderly
And chose what not to say,

The while, with prodigality,
She gave herself away.

Those guarding her, did not once guess
They helped her set the stage
On which she won from them her will,
Release from custom's cage.

She hand-picked the small audience,
Composed the comedy,
Designed her costume, virginal,
With deadly irony.

Then, from the safety of her home,
She played her eccentric part,
Enduring ridicule to gain
Freedom to learn her art.

Sometimes she had to break the bounds
Which she had drawn herself,
Needing to let the poet slip
The guise of spinster elf.

She asked advice from Higginson.
He told her where she erred.
She meekly thanked him for his laws
And never changed a word.

She scuttled through the hedge to Sue,
Thrust kingdoms in her hand,
And fled the knowledge that she, too,
Would fail to understand.

Exposure set her gift at risk.
To guard her writing, she
Retired into her legend,
Freakish anonymity.

The ploy grew more elaborate,
The rules more limiting.
At last, she kept within her room
Where she could sit and sing

The truth of her humanity,
Marking how dawns occur,
Threading love's maze with metaphor,
Each line her signature.

So she wove ambiguities
As blinding as the sun,
Reading the riddle of herself
Softly to everyone.

Jean Little